CHILDREN
LEARNING GEOMETRY

The cover design is suggested by the diagram for Euclid Bk 1 Prop. 5, once called the pons asinorum *or Bridge of Asses. It was said that a pupil who crossed the bridge by learning this theorem could continue the study of geometry with confidence.*

CHILDREN LEARNING GEOMETRY

**Foundation Activities in Shape
(5–9)**

A handbook for teachers

Edited for members of the Mathematical
Education Section of the National
Association of Teachers in Further
and Higher Education

by

J. A. Glenn

Illustrated by
David Parkins

Harper & Row, Publishers

London   New York   Hagerstown   San Francisco

Copyright © 1979 Harper and Row
Ltd

First published 1979
Harper & Row Ltd
28 Tavistock Street
London WC2E 7PN

British Library Cataloguing in Publication Data

Children learning geometry.
  1. Geometry – Study and teaching
     (Elementary)
  I. Glenn, John Albert
  II. National Association of
     Teachers in Further and Higher
     Education. *Mathematics Education
     Division*
  372.7'3   QA461

ISBN 0 06 318118 5 cased
     0 06 318119 3 paperback

Typeset by Input Typesetting Ltd
Printed and bound by The Garden
City Press Ltd, Letchworth

Other publications by members of the Mathematical Education Section:

Edited by K. L. Gardner *et al.*, published by Oxford University Press

Children Using Mathematics (1971)

Edited by J. A. Glenn, published by Harper and Row

Teaching Primary Mathematics : Strategy and Evaluation (1977)

The Third R : Towards a Numerate Society (1978)

Some young mathematicians first indicate their talents by their skill at geometry. Infants may show this by an unusual ability with bricks, or by making patterns in art, or by their skill with logi-blocks. Initially this may be intuitive, but later the young mathematicians stand apart from the young artists by their ability to verbalise their experiences and to discuss what would happen if the conditions were varied. Over recent years, the amount of geometry in primary schools has increased: thus the opportunities for the gifted to develop and the responsibilities on the teacher to appreciate what is happening have increased correspondingly.

Gifted Children in Middle and Comprehensive Schools, HMSO, 1977

Contents

Preface

This book, like its three predecessors, is a contribution to mathematical education made by members of the Mathematical Education Section of the National Association of Teachers in Further and Higher Education. It is written directly for practising or intending teachers of children in the 5-9 age range. It does not assume an interest in academic mathematics, although we have had in mind the teacher who may take over responsibility for the mathematical programme of a primary school. We have tried to make it mathematically respectable yet intelligible to the general professional reader who is not a mathematician, and we also offer it to teachers of more formal geometry as an example of the informal intuitive foundations of knowledge and experience on which later and more elaborate structures can be built. It is part of our overall thesis that mathematical education often fails because these foundations are inadequate or lacking.

The text has been compiled and edited by J. A. Glenn of the former Kesteven College of Education, from material submitted by present or former members of the Section, too many to be named individually. A major contribution, setting the general approach of the whole work, was prepared by

Jack Forster
John Mills
John Walker

All three now belong to the Faculty of Education of the University of Warwick.

The Section is grateful to the Nuffield Mathematics Continuation Fund Committee for a grant meeting the expenses of preparing the manuscript, and to Sheila Harris for typing the final draft.

J. A. Glenn and Harper & Row would like to express their thanks to the following for their help with the manuscript: Hilda Doran, Shirley Coker, Richard Harvey and Peter Dean.

Check-list of mathematical terms

Although this book is written for teachers, we try to avoid the technical language of mathematics and educational theory except where ordinary language fails us. We give below the mathematical vocabulary of the entire text, apart from the appendix devoted to later work. Some of the words like 'hypotenuse' appear but once in passing, others like 'tangram' are explained when used. The rest are used on the assumption that they will be intelligible in context. We assure readers that this list is only given for the benefit of their colleagues.

acute	net	right angle
angle	noncommutative	rotation
bilateral	obtuse	scalene
bisector	octagon	set
circumference	ordering (relation)	sphere
congruent	parallel	square
cube	parallelogram	straight (angle)
cuboid	pentagon	subtended
cylinder	perpendicular	surface
diagonal	perspective	symmetry
equidistant	plane	tangram
equilateral	polygon	tessellation
equivalent	point	tetrahedron
ellipse	prism	three-dimensional
geoboard	projection	transformation
hexagon	pyramid	translation
horizontal	quadrilateral	trapezium
hypotenuse	radius	trapezoid
isosceles	rectangle	triangle
line	re-entrant	two-dimensional
midpoint	reflection	vertex
multibase	rhombus	vertical

Introduction to the activities

1. Geometry and the early school years

Children and the language of mathematics

If children are to do mathematics they must learn the language of mathematics. This at once presents a difficulty that concerns us all. Anyone who has tried to prepare written material for mathematical or scientific studies in primary schools sooner or later comes up against the inevitable criticism. The children, one is told, can do the calculations or perform the experiments easily enough, but they cannot read the problem or understand the instructions.

Looking at some of the work in print, one can see the force of the criticism, but the question arises whether or not some traditional approaches to reading make any form of 'technical' writing for children almost impossible. If a book has a drawing labelled

This is a hexagon

or the pupil has a workcard which begins

Ask your teacher for a thermometer

then surely no further simplification of these two sentences is possible. On the other hand, those who object to the use of such words as hexagon and thermometer in printed material can easily show, by asking a child to read the sentences aloud, that the reader stumbles as expected. There are three points to be made and developed.

The first is that, although it is likely that only a minority of children in the early years of school have actually seen a live pig or even a hen, every child in every school in the country can not only see a diagram of a hexagon, but, much more important, can handle cut-outs and objects having the shape of a hexagon, can draw hexagons and make them up with jointed or pivoted strips. That is, the word can be the label of a completely familiar object as common in the classroom as objects at home or school called by such polysyllabic names as

television

refrigerator

tomato

radiator

By contrast, pigs may be as literary and fabulous as dragons. There is a difference, of course. There must be few children who come to school unable to use the words *tomato* and *television*; but there are very few indeed who already know what a hexagon is. Moreover, there are many adults unfamiliar with the word. So *hexagon* is a hard word, and is not likely to appear in a school's reading scheme. It is not included in the two main classes of words found in reading schemes, the straightforward phonetic like *pig* and the 'look-say' word which is chosen because it is presumably known and used in speech before the child begins to read. Such words need to be kept under review. One well-known scheme in use as late as the 1960s included, for instance, the word *aeroplane*, which today, like *omnibus* and *cinematograph*, has almost disappeared from ordinary use.

The actual text of a reading scheme is devised to be read, and not to convey information or give instructions, which are among the principal uses of language. This is unavoidable during the very early stages of reading, but the schemes rarely allow for the transition to more specialized or even technical uses. These uses are, however, found more commonly in schools than in many other places. Where else do people spend much of their time working with books on mathematics, science, geography ... on studies, that is, with their own special vocabularies unheard in shops and on street corners? The preliminary conclusion seems to be that the vocabularies of reading schemes should include the words that the children will need for their other studies. If the school is to do something in mathematics more demanding than addition and subtraction, the child must learn to call a hexagon a hexagon.

This at once brings us to the second point we wish to make. The vocabulary we are after only takes its meaning in context: it could hardly fit into a reading scheme as such. We need another approach. The final conclusion, which seems to be unavoidable, is that we should treat the first appearances of a necessary technical word or expression in a text or a lesson as an exercise in reading and comprehension, linking it always with something the child can see, draw, make, handle, or in some way do. This goes not only for any age group whose members have reading difficulties, but for all children as a check on their use of language. The writer's job is, then, to avoid the unnecessary technicality and the unfamiliar construction: if he fails in this his work is indeed beyond the scope of the children.

Given such a strategy, normal children readily learn that quadrilateral, pentagon, and hexagon are the names of polygons, as easily as they learn that ash, elm, and oak are the names of trees. The difference, perhaps, is that they will recognize the first set more readily.

This brings us to the third point, which at first seems to take us a long way from our job in teaching mathematics, but is in fact central to it. We have suggested that words such as tetrahedron and trapezium need be no more difficult than helicopter and elephant: children can learn to read them by 'look-say' methods and they convey an immediate concept. The geometrical objects themselves can become familiar and the children soon learn to decode the visual patterns of letters that label them. Teachers who use flash cards could include words such as these after the children have seen and handled the shapes.

But there are other kinds of language, most easily recognized outside mathematics. Compare these two sentences, chosen to be as far from mathematics as possible.

The beautiful princess waited on the
battlements till she saw the handsome
prince and the ancient magician disappear

from sight on the enchanted island.

Man can find himself only in death, which is
his true life.

The first sentence contains many more 'hard' words than the second, and readers might like to determine the 'readability index' for each. But once the printed letters are decoded into the words of the spoken language – that is, once they are read – the first passage becomes immediately intelligible to any young child not from a culturally deprived home. This is certainly not true of the second: a seven-year-old could easily read it, but would only be 'barking at print'.

It is sentences of the second kind that cause a lot of the trouble in mathematics teaching. We can deal with 'rhombus' or 'tetrahedron' by simple demonstration, but to get a response to questions such as

In what ways are the shapes in this list the same?

requires careful and patient preparation as the children's minds begin to take unaccustomed paths. We hope that this book will help with both languages.

We owe it to the reader to explain our own use of two technical words that we cannot easily replace with others. These are 'formal' and 'concept'. By formal, we mean considered independently of any actual picture or material representation. The geometrical ideas we develop are firmly based on drawings and solid objects, and are thus *informal*. By concept, we mean an idea conceived in the mind by the fertilization of learning and experience. The child's experiences will include the school work which the teacher's skill can enrich. A 'concept' in our use of the word cannot be taught, although good teaching both helps in its formation and develops it by discussion.

On looking at shape

The word geometry brings an instant mental response from those adults for whom it has any meaning at all. Geometry is about perpendicular bisectors, angles subtended at the centres of circles, congruent triangles and the square-on-the-hypotenuse. Because of this we tried to keep the word out of the title of this book, but found no other that was not equally misleading. We were concerned with the child's concept of space, but this word 'space' is now inseparable from science fiction and rocketry. We wanted the children to look at shape, but this concept was too general. We wanted them to look at shape in a very special sort of way, as made up of lines or surfaces or solids, yet to see these things through the child's eye, not the mathematician's.

Many quite elementary books sometimes assume that the learner can already see and think mathematically. They begin with simple concepts and develop them by a treatment that avoids formal reasoning, but takes it for granted that the child is capable of the abstract thinking that makes the apparently simple concepts possible in the first place. Young children do not yet think mathematically and they need help in beginning to do so, in learning to look at the world around them. For some of them, awareness of abstract spatial relationships and even formal geometrical reasoning, if it should ever be needed, will become possible.

Many children now grown up never got far along this road, and it is no longer seriously argued that the traditional school courses were able to help them very much. It is less frequently admitted that most people, adults living useful and productive lives, have very little need for formal geometry. A few do, of course, often in a rather limited and special context that can be applied to navigation, surveying, or engineering training. The difficulties some students or apprentices have in making progress in these activities lead their instructors to criticize schools in the mass, demanding for all children a syllabus that includes the geometrical knowledge held to be necessary for the few.

The problem in its very widest and most general sense is clearly one that has never been solved, for which all proposed and attempted solutions have failed. An ideal education, it is said, enriches and satisfies the mind, allows all citizens to develop their aptitudes and interests, helps them to live in a physical world of which they have some understanding, playing a useful part in a society whose structures are both stable and just.

Our immediate problems are all the more frustrating in that they seem trivial against this utopian fantasy. If only we could get the school leavers to add up properly, we should all be that much at least better off! Our recent publication, *The Third R: Towards a Numerate Society* (Harper and Row, 1978), argued that some (but not, of course, all) of the difficulties in number skills among otherwise normal children arise during early school days before computation proper is taught. We are now trying to deal with early ideas of geometry.

We have tried to keep our use of the word geometry at this stage clear of both its traditional and more modern academic forms, and apart from a knowledge of the few words in the check-list we do not call for skill in either on the part of our readers. For the purposes of this book, written as it is for the teachers of children in the age range five to nine, formal geometry is a systematic study of shape that becomes possible *after* children have learned to look at shape geometrically. The activities described are intended to lay the foundations; they are a source of material from which each teacher can develop a programme to suit the needs of children somewhere in the range, giving them a way of using their eyes and their fingers that day-to-day living rarely provides.

What we mean by looking at space and shape geometrically is best seen by referring to the activities themselves. Normally we do not look at things in any particular way; we simply look at them. Only deliberate introspection tells us (often in inescapably stilted language) what it is we are doing. Do we consciously use our eyes to identify by its distinctive shape a cup of tea from among the many things on a table, to locate it and control the movement of our fingers towards it? Of course not: we simply pick it up and drink.

We do, nevertheless, speak of looking at things through the eye of the artist, and it is an important and relatively successful aspect of schoolwork that we try to teach children to do just this. They do not all become artists, but at least they have a chance of responding to the artist's vision. In a similar way, not everyone becomes a mathematician, but we should all gain if, at times, we could adopt those ways of thinking that characterize mathematics.

These early stages in mathematics are accessible to all but a few and can be presented in a way that extends our use of language and our intellectual appreciation of the structure of the world of things. From that point the foundations are there for any later development. Whether the average ten-year-old should begin a systematic study of geometrical notions may not be certain, but whether the average nine-year-old should is clearer. The answer, in general, is no: there are far too many preliminary ideas and concepts that call for formation first. Some of them are introduced in this book.

We do try not to force our opinions onto the teacher, but in making explicit suggestions for using and extending our activities we hope that many will be willling to use this book as we have planned. For all that, it is not a textbook of primary geometry but a source book of geometrical thinking, and the material is presented so that the teacher can decide how to put it to use.

Children and their world

No teacher of children in the 5-9 age group, especially one not yet free of the Euclidean connotations of the word, is likely to put geometry on a list of 'subjects' that ought to be taught, even if teaching in a school that still divides and timetables its work in this way. Seen, however, as one of the ways in which children become aware of their environment, geometric activity takes its place among the many activities that fill the school day. Children become aware of environment through interaction with it, through the interpretations their brains make of the impulses that arrive from their six senses. The truly fundamental operations of the brain in fitting together the sense data into a coherent picture start at birth and are substantially complete by the time the child begins to speak; but from this point onwards the child is in intelligent communication with others and as a human being begins to have available the collective knowledge and skill of society.

'Geometrical' activity is involved in refining the raw data our senses feed in – information about space, shape, and movement that helps us to think usefully about what we see and feel. What is *seen* is space and shape, colour and movement. What is *felt* is texture, but the feeling and seeing together join forces with the kinaesthetic sense that tells us how our limbs and fingers are positioned. These three senses allow us to place ourselves in space and become aware of shape, of size, of mass, of movement, of effort.

In thinking geometrically we concern ourselves with shape and size and movement, rather than colour or texture or mass, and what we hear or smell or taste is not taken into account at all. The job of primary education is to deal with the whole environment of the child; but it is useful and convenient on occasion to separate some of the factors that contribute. Shape, size, and movement are interesting to discuss, because in them we have an almost exact correlation of two quite different senses. What we see when we look at an object is normally confirmed by what we feel if we touch it. One of the objects of the activities we describe is to use this correlation of two senses to develop perception in both. We want children to use their eyes and develop skills with their fingers. This is a very human correlation, and it is interesting to compare it with the behaviour of bats and dolphins, who seem to correlate hearing rather than seeing with their kinaesthetic sense.

The task of the primary school

It is wrong to emphasize geometric thinking or any other specific activity at the expense of what many would consider to be the main job of the primary teacher. They would say that the aim of a school is not only to teach children but to develop in them an awareness and understanding of other people and an ability to live and work together. Attitudes matter as much as skills. This implies talking together, discussing, explaining, agreeing, disagreeing, convincing, and being convinced. It implies a lot more, of course, but language and communication help to make society possible. We also want our children to react actively to the physical world, both of nature and of man. We want them to enquire about it, to notice things, to be able to describe them, and to link them together in their minds. We hope that young children will go on wanting to know why things happen as they do. Everyone who manages to keep intellectual curiosity regrets its absence among older pupils who lose it.

It seems pretentious to say that geometry can be of value in helping forward these ends, but remember we are now giving this name to a whole range of classroom activities that do call on the child to look, to handle, to discuss, to record. These activities are concerned with space and movement, with concentrating the child's mind on the shape and position of objects rather than on the objects themselves, and it is in this sense that they are geometrical. Looking well ahead, the skills we are hoping to generate can be, for the child who responds to them, the foundation for later deeper and more systematic knowledge, especially if the child happens to opt for a continuing mathematical education or has some future professional need.

At this early stage, however, we are merely asking that the children should become explicitly aware of the space they live in, of the shapes and sizes of things, and of the ways in which they fit together, the way things move and change position or direction. And in doing this the children are taking their first controlled lessons in abstraction, in looking at a heuristically simplified world to focus on geometrical properties that are independent of texture and colour, although we may use texture and colour to emphasize them. This, and only this, is what we mean by 'geometry' with the 5-9 age group. It does not follow that all readers will agree, but if they do not this book will not help them.

The fundamental objects of geometry in our use of the word are not points and lines and triangles, but the ordinary solid three-dimensional objects of our three-dimensional space. The child comes to school with a good practical working knowledge of this world, but instead of building on it we tend to force all subsequent learning into the two-dimensional abstractions of letters, numerals, words, sums, pictures, and diagrams. Most organized knowledge *is* two-dimensional in this sense, but it is part of the school's job to make the transition.

We might also add, although it is some parents rather than teachers who need to be persuaded here, that it is certainly not part of a primary school's function to prepare children for a job. If only for this reason, we must be cautious about all claims for the technical utility of what we are doing, which are made in the hope of providing incentive. If our geometry is not interesting for its own sake, it is not worth the effort of general study. Such 'applications' as there are of geometry are either like the design of the fifty pence coin and the steering linkages of a car, too subtle for young children, or else, like the too often expounded 3 : 4 : 5 triangle, *ad hoc* scraps of information taken from some later stage whose practical interest is soon exhausted. Nor should we put history into reverse to justify our lessons, although as teachers we are often tempted to do this. The bricklayer who wheels a barrowload of bricks and lays them in a straight course with the aid of a stretched cord is not, as one sometimes hears, 'applying the properties of circles and straight lines': he is engaged in an activity many centuries older than geometry. The circle took its name from the Greek word for a wheel, the geometric line from the Latin for a flaxen thread. Geometry abstracts, but can only begin in a society of already high technical achievement. Our job with this age group is to give the children of our own technological society the concrete experiences from which the abstractions can come.

At home and at school

Not the least of the difficulties faced by the teacher of five-year-old children is the wide difference in their home backgrounds, operating as they have been for five years on each child without the blending action of a shared school life. At this age the environmental differences are likely to outweigh innate differences of intelligence. We have said more about the background of reception classes in our report *Children Using Mathematics* (Oxford 1971). What is pertinent here is that, although children may come from homes without books and may never have had stories read to them, they must all have had some sort of opportunity to learn about space and shape.

They will all have handled things, have found that objects are rounded or have sharp projecting points, that some remain where they are put while others topple over or roll away out of sight. There are many questions they will never have put into words, which are the raw material of geometry. What is 'out of reach' and how far away does a thing have to be before it is? Why can a grown-up take a thing from a high shelf inaccessible to the child? What is the difference between the shapes you can make with dry sand and those you can make with mud? Why does water run away if the bowl is tipped up? Why do I make dirty footprints all over the floor on a wet day? Watch a small child get angry because a large box will not go through a half-open gate, or burst into tears because a ball thrown over a wall does not come back.

By the time the child begins school the spatial awareness implied by these questions is well developed operationally. The child acts in response to the situations that arise, but does not fit them into formal schemes of mathematics or science. Without the help of the teacher few children would learn that there are such schemes.

But we can only build on this foundation of natural learning if all the necessary stones are in position. For the fortunate child the early activities in this book only recapitulate and assemble earlier experiences, describing them in words that begin to put language to use; but for the less fortunate they could be an introduction to geometrical thinking as it begins to emerge from ordinary discourse.

We believe that the first four years or so of school life, as far as geometrical thinking is concerned, should be regarded as an extension of both experience and working vocabulary. We do not try to derive general statements (although we do not try to avoid a generality if it is obvious). If we ask a child to count the faces, edges, and vertices of a cube, it is only to help the cube to pass from a more or less familiar shape to one intensively inspected and handled. We do not try to arrive at a theorem about the faces, edges, and vertices of polyhedra. The word 'theorem', in fact, will not be used again in this book.

Perhaps we should say something about our decision not to go beyond the age of nine. It could well be that by this age a few children (but only a few) will be able to carry investigations to formally general conclusions. Our response to these children would be to direct them into more detailed study of the topics, to suggest for them other areas of related interest. The ability to generalize from the particular may be a sign of mental maturity, but from 5-9 the emotional and social development is what matters most, and if our activities are taken as intended they should contribute in a modest way to both. There is and must be a certain arbitrariness in this decision, but it seems that although many ten-year-olds can carry out work more systematically than our activities require, most nine-year-olds will find themselves stretched by them. The nine-year-olds, who will already have come a long way since they were five, still have a potential school career equal in length to their entire past life, and we need not rush. We are asking for careful study over a carefully delimited area.

We believe that this detailed study – detailed observation is perhaps the better expression – of a limited but carefully chosen range of shapes and topics related to them is one of the appropriate activities for developing mathematical understanding in young children. The group of H.M. Inspectors who prepared the recent survey report of the Department of Education and Science, *Primary Education in England* (September 1978), noted that primary children have of late shown a welcome improvement in numerical skills. Our aim is to see that this is accompanied by a growth of spatial insight in the mathematical sense, and for this reason we have made our approach to geometry almost entirely qualitative. Modern mathematics teaching tries to integrate its topics, but we are dealing with young children, some of whom may find number work difficult. Our treatment should, we hope, give them an opportunity for a new start (as indeed traditional geometry sometimes did for much older pupils). The synthesis into mathematics can come later. The activities that follow are offered through the teacher rather than directly to the children, in the hope that they will both develop the foundations for an important part of mathematics and provide an interesting and enjoyable experience.

2. The use of this book

The plan of the material

The working section of this book consists of a set of 50 topics described as geometrical activities and investigations. Given time and a group of staff in sympathy with one another, it is not difficult to devise an agreed programme of informal geometrical work to span the 5-9 age range. But interpreting this as the day-by-day lessons and activities of any given class is less straightforward.

We have adopted what seemed to be the only practicable way of getting the essential material into a form which is suitable for all age and ability groups of whatever background within the age range, and which does not duck from the responsibility of turning an item in a syllabus into detailed work for the children. We have written up the activities as suggestions for the teacher, inserting notes and comments into the text whenever necessary or helpful.

The decision to do this has proved a happy one. Instead of struggling to write for a hypothetical child and arriving, even if successful, at a piece of work too difficult for some and too trivial for others, we let the teacher know what we would like done, thus putting the procedure into the capable hands of the one person who knows how Hilary, age 7½, a non-reader but an irrepressible talker, is best given her instructions. In the event, the expedient has allowed us a scope and flexibility that no scheme written for children could achieve. Each activity is devoted to a topic that plays its part in developing the geometric theme, but we do not have to guess at the length of lessons or the span of Hilary's attention. We are writing for professionals who know more about children and classrooms than we do. We also assume that our readers will be familiar with the work of Piaget and others who have shown how children learn to use their concepts. Their findings are implicit in everything we suggest, but this is not the place to give an account of them.

We have let the topics take over. Some of the activities, clearly, can provide material for several weeks of work. Some of them suggest individual work for children, some suggest group activity, some are intended to be taken as a single lesson for the whole class, whatever the range of reading abilities. The Department's survey *Primary Education in England* (Sec. 5.65) notes the value of the class lesson in a set-up which is mainly group or individual work; and indeed we do at times, in our concern for the individual, forget that a class is an entity, a group to which the child needs to belong. But the activities do not force any one procedure. Because they avoid generalities and try to present material in a workable form, they give step-by-step instructions; but the interpretation of them is at the teacher's discretion, and they can be modified *secundum artem* to suit circumstances other than those implied by the actual wording. Our decision to stop at nine years can be seen in the light of this flexibility.

The activities are, it is true, arranged in an order of development and we have taken some care over this sequencing, but, if a teacher feels that a topic can be brought forward or ought to be delayed, this can easily be done. It is the teacher who gives (or writes) the instructions in the language the child can follow and, although we sometimes suggest wording for a workcard at the child's level, there is no question of the child's having to follow *our* directions.

We also want to make it quite clear that in spite of our recommended sequence, the 50 activities do not in any way form a continuous work scheme with each activity beginning as its predecessor ends. They are topics rather than prepared lessons and are intended to provide the essential geometric content of a total mathematics course, or, in less academic language, work in shape to go with work in number. Teachers may find only a dozen of them are appropriate to the work of the first two years, and in this age range we think it is better to postpone activities rather than try to do too much too soon. We have tried to make the material interesting, imaginative, even novel in presentation, even though the age group is working so far within the limits of the scope of modern mathematical education that we cannot hope to describe anything not done before. Each activity can be chosen and fitted in when and where the teacher pleases, and can be recapitulated or repeated in more detail if needed. Obviously, the earlier activities are for the younger children, and many of the later ones have extensions intended for the more able, but each is routed through the teacher. We have sometimes put together activities which could follow one another. On the other hand, we have deliberately separated some related activities, for example, 11 and 15, so that the second reminds the pupil of the first at a later date. Again, we have put a simple activity such as 49 near the end of the list as a relaxation exercise for an older class. Each activity as listed in the contents page has a subtitle in the text. This suggests an aim or content for the work described. The book is presented as a compendium of fully worked out suggestions for the use of schools: its ultimate dependence on the skill and competence of the reader as a teacher (although not necessarily as a mathematician) will, we hope, prove to be its greatest strength.

Strategy for the teacher

Although our activities are only suggestions for the consideration of teachers, it would be tedious to express all of them in too tentative a way, and we have not tried to avoid imperative constructions where it is simpler to use them. Readers of the activities are asked to interpret every imperative as a suggestion or hint, and to modify it as required in the light of the children's needs. The nine numbered paragraphs that follow give our suggested procedure.

1 Look quickly through the entire set before selecting any one activity, since the others may contain hints for extending or applying the work of the one chosen. This is, however, a source book and is not meant to be read from end to end at a sitting.

2 Select one or more topics which are capable of fitting into the time available. The activities are not intended to meet a regular time allotment of one hour per week or whatever: each is a small project to be worked at for as long as it provides interest, and can be laid aside or picked up as convenient, perhaps in another class or another year.

3 Read the activity through carefully, well in advance of beginning to use it, trying out anything that is unfamiliar or likely to cause difficulty. Some of the activities may call for materials not readily to hand in the classroom, or require the children to collect boxes or other objects before they can begin. Do not begin any activity without all the necessary apparatus and materials.

4 If an activity seems interesting or useful for one age or ability group but the suggested instructions imply another, consider whether it can be adapted. Activity 1, for example, asks the children to read a worksheet; but by using pictures only, small ones for individual or small groups, large ones for a large group, the entire activity can be taken orally with non-readers. One could introduce it with the story of 'The Three Bears'. It can then be repeated later when the children concerned can read.

5 Be prepared to bring a topic to an early conclusion if it is not going well, and allow it to run on if it proves fruitful. Remember, however, that the topics are not once-and-for-all investigations to be completed and put aside, but as far as possible 'open-ended' to be linked up to more advanced work later. If bright children get through an activity more quickly than expected, then *for this age range* we consider that further parallel examples and activities are better than attempts at generalization. Activity 9, for example, asks pupils to count and record the faces, vertices, and edges of a cube. Its natural extension would be to collect results from other simple polyhedra, but *not* a premature discussion of the numerical relation between these three counts. Do leave something of interest for more mature discovery! It is clear that here we have a situation, common in primary schools where the very brightest children are still awaiting recognition, that calls for the greatest professionalism on the part of the teacher. The books listed in the appendix (p. 124) should be of help.

6 Consider very carefully any new words or phrases that the activity, as it stands or any adaptation of it, will need to use. When these occur, there should be a pause for discussing the words, their spelling, and their use in the context. Make sure that each child concerned can use them, can read them aloud, can show examples, or otherwise demonstrate a grasp of the meanings. And, most important, the words or expressions could be brought up in class several times within the next few days and thereafter kept in use. Children forget new words they do not use as adults forget the vocabulary of a foreign language.

7 Schools are often asked to provide facilities for students and others investigating educational matters, and we strongly recommend these activities for experimental set-ups in class, rather than the basic subjects whose acquisition may be put at risk. Consider the pedagogic questions:

What is the optimum size of a small
working group?

What are the advantages or disadvantages
of partnering a poor reader with an able child?

Does a 'friendship group' work better than a
group formed in any other way?

One can learn much about these and similar questions by trying out number work with a class, but as a result a child may fail to learn skills necessary for progress. If, on the other hand, evaluation of one of our activities shows that children in a trial grouping have failed to grasp a geometrical concept, the activity or a modification of it can easily be produced for them under different conditions of learning. No permanent harm has then been done by using children as guinea pigs.

8 Where practical skills are called for, from drawing up tables of data to assembling structures of rods, cardboard, or wood, try to get each child working as neatly and effectively as possible. We do not wish each task to become a laborious exercise in a skill not properly developed, but at least it should help to improve manipulative abilities. We see no harm in asking a child to repeat a slapdash construction done well below known aptitude. But may we add that the teacher's own demonstration items, if a large-scale class diagram or construction is called for, should themselves be exemplary?

Do not hesitate to use an activity known to have been done before, perhaps in a previous year. In this case introduce it by a brief recapitulation (which may well show, if the work was premature, that it has been almost entirely forgotten) and tell the children that they are going to extend the work done. Since the geometrical concepts of the activities are intended to be more or less completely understood and retained by the nine-year-old, recapitulation and parallel activities are essential. Some of the activities contain extensions that are suitable only for a second run through.

9 Keep a record which covers the progress of a pupil through the age group, so that whoever takes over at the end of it knows what has been done. Keeping records is often an unrewarding chore whose end product is rarely examined or used. If our scheme is adopted, one needs a set of cards with the activity numbers 1–50 and enough room for the record as agreed by staff.

All that is needed is a tick to show that something has been done, although some schools would prefer a date. An activity can be ticked or dated more than once where it is capable of being worked over again in a modified or extended form, or where its work is, by agreement, split over more than one year. A comment can be made if an activity is evaluative. Another class teacher can see what has been done by a glance at the card and book together, planning progression from that point.

Name ————————————————————————————————

Activity		Activity
1		26
2		27
3		28
:		:
:		:
25		50

A note for headteachers

Although this book claims to be written for the teacher who has charge of children somewhere in the age range 5-9, it has no doubt become clear to the reader that it is really written for the school (or even schools) spanning this period in the child's life. It calls for some degree of cooperation between classes, in that it does not give a year-by-year syllabus but a four- or five-year programme to be considered as a whole, by a team of teachers who are in broad agreement with its approach. If the suggestions for posts of special subject responsibility, such as are discussed explicitly for mathematics in the Department of Education and Science report *Primary Education in England* (Chapter 8, Section 46), ever become fully implemented, there could be widespread developments in planned teaching over age ranges in this way. It should then become much easier to get a scheme such as ours into operation. This will be particularly true about our suggestions for keeping records. There are also implications for post-primary education that are mentioned in Appendix II.

Geometrical activities and investigations

1 The language of shape: the use of descriptive words.

> This activity is a possible starting point for young children. It aims to put a particular kind of vocabulary to use, and to help pupils recognize those attributes that eventually, in a more specialized context, become part of the study of mathematics. It can begin when children are ready to read sentences such as those given, but the lesson in reading is to be part of the lesson in 'geometry'. We do not wait until the children have learned to read in some other context.

Begin this work by discussing people and objects in ordinary language chosen for its relevance to descriptions of shape or size. Use sentence cards and pictures drawn as the examples shown on the worksheet, although only simple outlines are needed. Use different constructions for the descriptive sentences. Here are typical sentences:

Here is a tall man.

This is a fat boy.

This woman is thin.

Here is a girl. She is a little girl.

Consolidate and extend the work with many similar sheets showing trees, houses, animals, motorcars, and so on, chosen to bring in words such as:

wide	high	large	small
big	broad	long	narrow

If possible take the children out of doors and discuss whatever can be seen in terms of shape and size. Point to objects such as trees or buildings and ask questions such as

Is that tree as tall as that building?

Can you see a taller tree?

Which is the highest building in sight?

This is an opportunity to discuss comparative and superlative forms of adjectives.

For able children who are fluent speakers a short session of this work will act as a rapid check on their abilities. For the slower learner it is important that they should use English in less colloquial modes since some of them may not get the opportunity at home. Fluent speech is socially more important than an eventual knowledge of mathematics. It is not necessary for children to agree on what is said or written so long as they can justify themselves in discussion.

The worksheet that follows is for the child who can write the sentences as well as read them. It may be necessary to go over the sheet verbally, since it is easier for the child to write 'he is a fat man' than to follow the instructions. We have already suggested on p. 26 that the work can be done verbally with slow readers.

Work Sheet for Activity 1 (written exercise)

Here are some pictures of people. Write a sentence under each picture using words like:

tall	fat	thin	short	little	big

One sentence is written for you to show you what to do.

this is a tall man

2 Size and shape: specific and general description

This work begins to clear up, for the purposes of mathematics, the ambiguities of the words 'size' and 'shape' as we commonly use them. This use, of course, is quite correct in terms of English idiom, but is not what is later needed in geometry. We have the concept of size and the two concepts of a general shape and a specific shape. All cars have the general shape we recognize as 'car' and all dogs have a different general shape from cats. In geometry triangles have a different general shape from rectangles. All maps of the British Isles, however, have the same specific shape, whatever their size or colour.

Prepare a large chart showing at least three drawings of the same person or object, differing only in scale. Squared paper may be used to enlarge an outline but avoid arranging the drawings in perspective so that they look as if they are the same size but diminished by distance. This can easily be checked by trying to draw 'vanishing lines' through their heads and feet. If you succeed, the drawings could be misleading, as the inset figure shows.

Ask questions such as

Do you think these are pictures of the same girl?

Are the pictures the same shape?

What has changed?

It may, as p. 32 suggests, be necessary to 'talk around' these questions before they are understood.

When the situation is clear, summarize the discussion with a statement such as

These pictures have exactly the same shape but they do vary in size.

Consolidate and extend by handling and discussing dolls and scale model toys, but now include a few objects that have the formal shapes of cuboids and spheres. This simply means that one introduces objects such as break-fast food packets and balls among those being handled and discussed. Children are likely to reach agreement that all balls are the same shape even when different in size. The breakfast food packets, since their propor-tions vary, will present much more difficulty. Is a tall thin box the same shape as a short squat one? We want to say that they are both cuboids : they have the same general but different specific shapes. Can such a discussion be 'processed' by the teacher? This is a decision to be made in the light of the circumstances.

3 The use of language: further practice in description

Children should continue with the use of language that includes but does not overemphasize terms that will later be important in mathematics. Teachers who wish to do so may now introduce the word 'set', at this stage simply as a convenient synonym for a collec-tion of objects.

Have collections of objects such as small dolls, Dinky toys, buttons, leaves, shells, or stones and get children to sort them in trays, within hoops, or in closed loops drawn on sheets of paper. Check that the children understand instructions such as

Everything in this hoop must be a car.

Encourage children to talk about the sets, asking questions that include reference to shape and size, using adjectives in all their forms.

Are they all cars in this set?

Have you got a favourite car?

Is your favourite car the largest one?

Can you show me the smallest car?

How are all the cars alike?

What is the difference between these two?

This model van is the same size as this model car.

Is the van really the same size as the car?

Say what you can about this set of balls. How does the smallest differ from the largest?

Consolidate and extend the work by asking children to relate different objects in speech and writing. Collections of pictures are useful here, used by small working groups of children. For example, a child can put a picture on the table (of a small boy for example). Another puts a picture of a large dog near it, and a third describes the situation.

The teacher or another pupil can now change one of the pictures or both. The changes should include two pictures of the same object differing only in size and could also include two of the same shape and size. Advertising leaflets are a useful source of pictures.

4 Looking at cubes: comparison of similar objects

The children are asked to look more closely at one set of objects. This could be, if they can be collected, a set of models of different sizes of the same object, such as a car, but it is not likely that a sufficient range is available. It is nevertheless important to see that the relationships being investigated apply to all objects and not only 'mathematical' ones. The work is better done by small groups of children under teacher supervision.

Make a set or sets of at least six cubes from strong card. Two should be of the same size, the rest of different sizes. (Making the cubes could be a practical activity for older children.) The cubes will have many uses later, and should be kept with other shapes so that the pupils have to sort them out before they begin. They should be painted in different colours so that they can be referred to without ambiguity. A set could also be made by painting a few multibase arithmetic blocks if nobody objects to this extended use.

Discuss the ways in which the cubes differ. Are they the same size? Are they the same shape? Record using arrow diagrams, which can be introduced here if the children have not yet met them in their number work. The 'arrow' is simply a line linking two or more words, numbers, or pictures with an arrow marked on it to show the direction in which we are reading.

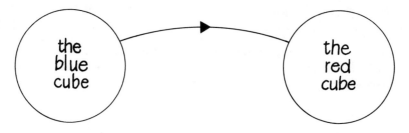

Ask what the arrow 'says'. Here, for example, it could say, with chosen cubes

is the same size as

or

is the same shape as

or

is the same size and shape as

By choosing another pair the arrow could read

is smaller than

is larger than

Extend by making up phrase cards of a suitable size which can be read as complete sentences when put between two cubes or some other shapes.

Example:

is the same size as	is the same shape as
is smaller than	is larger than

If possible, use these cards and the objects with children individually as a test of comprehension. They not only read the words; they show that they understand the context in which the words are used.

5 Ordering by size: sorting by a single attribute

The words 'shape' and 'size' have been used in describing objects. We are now going to arrange objects in order of size. The concept of an 'ordering relationship' is fundamental to later mathematical thinking, but arises quite naturally, primarily from the sort of work on comparative adjectives that arises in Activity 1. The work is intended to be done with a small group, but by using large cubes the teacher could give a class demonstration.

Using the set of cubes, ask a child to pick out the smallest. Put the smallest on the table, and ask a child to pick the next larger cube. Put this one down near the first, and repeat until all the cubes are down in a row. Ask what has been done.

The cubes have been arranged in order of size

Repeat the process, but starting with the largest cube. This again arranges them in order of size. Ask what the arrow would say if it linked up the cubes as they were laid out. It would either say

is smaller than

or

is larger than

according to the cube chosen as the start. It is this choice that determines the relationship that links each cube to its successor.

There are two questions that could be put and discussed as part of the activity; but possibly only to more able children and even then only on a later run through.

What happens if two cubes happen to be the same size?

How many cubes are wanted before I can set them in order?

Clearly the relation is established once two cubes are set out if they are of different sizes.

Set out two cubes and ask what the arrangement 'says'. By choosing the cubes suitably the children can continue the pattern of order in various ways. For example, the arrangement below reads 'the left cube is smaller than the right cube'.

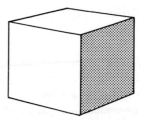

The same pattern may be continued with a smaller cube to the left, a larger to the right, or an intermediate cube in between so that a growing series of cubes is set out. Clues may be needed before the children see all three possibilities.

The use of 'left' and 'right' can obviously cause difficulties, particularly if a teacher is standing in front of the class. By saying 'the cube on this side' with a suitable gesture, the trouble is by-passed, but the problem remains. It could be better to say 'on my left' or 'on your left', again with a gesture, or even to say 'hold up your left hand' before saying 'on your left'. This could help children who confuse the two words 'left' and 'right'. Obviously this difficulty cannot be cleared up in a single lesson, and with some people it persists into adult life.

Extend the activity by asking the children to put one cube on top of another to build a tower. If this is done is it as easy to start with the smallest as with the largest? Children will soon find that one arrangement topples over, and will (much later) learn the word 'stability'. Any child who has played with bricks as a toddler will see the difficulty at once, but some children need every opportunity to handle material of this kind in a controlled way.

The work can be consolidated by devising simple games using phrase cards and sets of cubes. Multibase arithmetic blocks are convenient for the purpose.

Example:

Share out a set of cubes among four or six players.

Have a stack of phrase cards such as

is smaller than	is the same size as

face downwards between them. The first player turns up a card and puts down a cube. The next places the card by the cube and adds a cube to complete a sentence, then turns up the next card. The third player uses this new card and adds a cube to continue a chain of relationships, and so on;

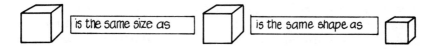

The teacher can easily extend the rules to suit the pupils. Note that the second card can be used between *all* cubes.

6 Evaluation (i)

The teacher may wish to check that children have linked the activities together in their minds and are beginning to grasp the concepts at the level discussed. The children should be able to follow instructions such as those given for the teacher here, either put verbally or discussed verbally after being written in a form to suit their reading ability, and they should be able to illustrate their answers by sorting and arranging apparatus or models.

1 One can have sets of objects which are the same size and shape. Give some examples.

2 Give examples of classification groups, of things such as dogs that are readily distinguishable one from the other, but which are described by the one noun.

3 Make a list of things that come in various sizes, although they all have

a) nearly the same shape

b) exactly the same shape

4 Given a set of objects, state a property that enables us to put them in order, and demonstrate with a suitable set.

Most common nouns (in the grammatical sense) serve to answer question 2. All classrooms will probably contain a wide assortment of packets, boxes, structured and number apparatus to illustrate the others. Although, of course, any set of objects can be put into some sort of order, such as order of preference, only an ordering relationship such as 'is smaller than' will do this uniquely. The objects are then arranged in the *same* order each time, and each child should be able to arrive at this.

This activity extends the teacher rather than the child! The evaluation process links with our final comment on page 28. The four exercises here given in language suited to the teacher, however one works at the vocabulary and constructions, are unlikely to be understood in writing by children not exceptionally mature. A box of scissors or plastic cubes shows examples of the set in question 1, but it could be quite difficult for a child to see what is wanted unless 'talked through' the instructions, however worded. There is no substitute for this, and children whose home backgrounds do not give them the chance to talk about general ideas are dependent on their schools.

The problem can be by-passed but not solved by using prepared sheets of drawings. A sheet showing several spoons, several cups, and so on, given with the instruction to 'draw loops round' things which have the same size and shape, or with suitably scaled drawings, things with the same shape but different sizes, would probably cause little trouble. A similar sheet for the second task could give outlines of different dogs, cats, and so on with the instruction to colour in the set of all dogs.

This approach will work and may be a valuable interim measure, but our final aim must be to get the pupil to respond to general concepts.

7 Looking and seeing: close observation of a solid

We often tell children to 'use their eyes', usually when we want them to see what happens to be obvious to ourselves. It took talented artists several thousand years before they devised the conventions of perspective, as distinct from drawing what we know about what we see. The activity below helps the children to 'use their eyes', and practises the skills of perception that in later life make it possible for them to understand diagrams and technical drawing.

Make a few cardboard 10 cm cubes (or use base 10 arithmetic blocks). Let a group of children stick a cut-out picture on each face of a cube.

One could once buy sheets of brightly coloured 'scraps' for cutting out and sticking into albums and these are now reappearing in the shops, but failing these, characters from comic strips will do. It is difficult to find suitable pictures the right size in magazines, although it is no doubt good for the children to search for them. Another cheap and abundant source of suitable brightly coloured pictures and motifs is the odd roll or roll-end of kitchen and nursery wallpaper, one of which can provide as many identical pictures as any class is likely to need. Some designs of wrapping paper sold in sheets are also suitable.

Ask how many pictures were used for each cube. Write the name of each object on a card, and put the cards on the table near the cube.

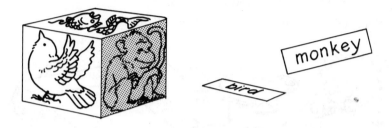

Now discuss which pictures can be seen or not seen by the group standing round the cube, asking such questions as

What pictures can you see?

Can you hold up the name cards of the pictures you can see?

Who can see only two pictures?

Who can see three?

Who can see four?

Is there a picture nobody can see?

Can you put yourself so that you can only see one?

Turn the cube over and try again, and try to get the groups to come to conclusions. Some of the questions are obviously addressed to individuals. Small children will naturally dodge their heads from side to side to see more. It will help if the children look at the cube through a 'telescope' made by curling their hands. The conclusions, of course, are about the number of faces that can be seen at any one time.

8   Shape and space: fitting things into spaces

This is a discussion using any suitable activity that comes to hand by way of example. We choose packing a suitcase. We are now looking at the spaces *between* objects, and asking what objects could occupy them. We want the children to see one of the ways in which shapes matter.

A useful discussion can begin with questions and comments:

Have you ever watched Mummy pack a suitcase for your holidays?

Does it hold everything you want to take?

Will it take a teddy bear when it is nearly full?

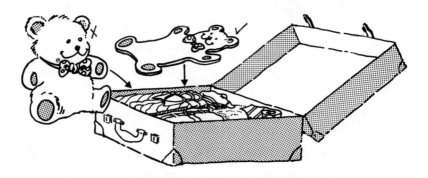

If Teddy were thin and flat like a shirt he would go in, but he is the wrong shape.

How many of you can sit inside a large hoop on the ground?

Try it.

Is there any space between you?

There is plenty of space, but it is not the right size or shape to take one more.

Consolidate and extend with activities that bring shapes together or match them up with spaces.

Examples:

1 Try putting glass marbles or pebbles in a jar. Is there any space left? It is worth asking the children to guess how much water (held in a similar jar) could be poured in before the spaces were all filled.

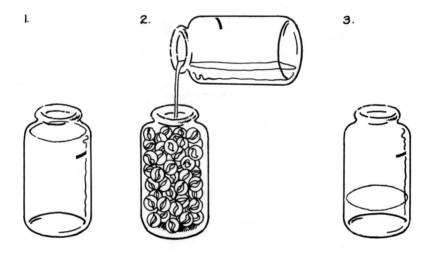

I.   2.   3.

By 'how much' in this context we mean 'a little' or a quarter or a half of the jar, and this might be the best way of putting the question. Perhaps a child could be asked to point before pouring to the expected final level.

2 Some classes now use attribute or 'logic' blocks for exercises in classifying by qualities that include shape and size. If these are at hand it is good for children to get used to packing them in the shaped containers provided, because they then match shapes with the spaces they occupy.

3 Some shapes, such as collections of matchboxes, fit together and leave no space between them. What shapes can the children find that do this?

9 Exploring the cube: detailed observation of a simple solid

This is a key activity, requiring the child to examine a given shape, a cube, in detail. Note that touch as well as sight is brought into play, and that the same structure is looked at in more than one way. The activity will take up several lessons, and will stretch the children. Teachers might prefer to bring forward Activity 11 as an interlude.

Ask each child to hold a wooden or well-made cardboard cube, turning it round to touch every part. The child should be asked to follow instructions such as these:

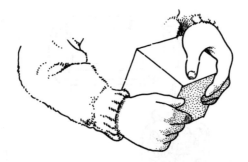

Close your eyes.

Run your fingers round the cube.

Put your hand on the bottom of the cube.

Now the top.

Now one of the sides.

How many sides has it got?

Run your finger across one of the sides.

How do you know when it finishes?

How many edges has each side?

The children can then open their eyes and follow the teacher's demonstration, which is intended to consolidate and extend what they have found out and check that the language is secure.

This is one of the sides of the cube.

If I turn it over it becomes the bottom or top.

Each side is flat, and has *edges*.

How many sides has the cube?

How many edges on each side?

Let us count *all* the edges.

The flat side is usually called a *face*.

Each face has four *edges*.

Is there any part of the cube we haven't named?

What about the corners? Feel the corners again on your cubes.

How many corners are there?

We now want to distinguish the various parts of the cube from one another. This can be done very pleasantly by labelling the faces and painting the corners. We have already stuck pictures or motifs onto the face of a cube in an earlier activity, and we are now going to extend the work. The children will stick a different picture on each face of the cube, having first decided how many pictures will be needed. If the children are in the early stages of reading it is worthwhile to produce and use name cards for each face, or names on additional slips which can be stuck on with the emblems.

The cube may have a moon face, a star face, a fish face, a flower face, a dog face, and a horse face. Different bright colours will be needed for the eight corners. Make sure that the colour is put on so that each of the three faces meeting at the vertex gets its fair share of colour. Suitable poster colours would be red, yellow, green, blue, brown, black, and grey. The child can now identify each corner and face and conclude:

A cube has six faces and eight corners.

Each face has a shape: it is called a *square*.

The children can now be given a duplicated sheet with six squares drawn on it (which need not be the same size as the faces of the cube) and given instructions:

Look at the star face.

How many colours can you see?

Paint on one of the squares the colours you can see on the star face, but do not draw the star.

Now repeat with the moon face – do you get a different pattern of colours?

How many patterns can you get in all?

Now ask the child to put a finger on one of the coloured corners, blue, for example:

How many faces can your finger touch if you press?

Can you touch three?

Name the faces that have a blue corner.

They can be referred to as 'the set of faces' and so recorded. The star face has a blue corner. The horse face has a blue corner. The fish face has a blue corner.

The work is repeated for the other corners; then we consider the relation between edges and corners.

Run your fingers along an edge.

How many edges run into the blue corner?

It may be necessary to demonstrate, since a phrase such as 'run into the blue corner' may not be understood. The child who has already counted faces, edges, and corners should now be ready for the questions that summarize the cube's structure.

Do three edges meet at each of the corners of this cube?

Do three faces meet at each corner of this cube?

The child should not only know the words *face*, *edge*, and *corner* (not vertex at this stage), but recognize them and count them. Different groups of pupils can use cubes of differing size so that the results can be seen to be independent of size. The work is not meant to be hurried, and as described is probably the limit of what can be attempted with young children.

10 Looking at shapes: extension to other solids

Without making the work more difficult, the previous activity can be extended by examining other simple shapes, such as cuboids, square pyramids, or triangular prisms. Plain wooden or cardboard models are needed, preferably given a coat of white emulsion paint.

Ask the children to paint each face a different colour.

Count the corners, and then press your finger onto each one in turn.

How many colours can you touch?

Record them for each corner. Set diagrams can be used : there are six altogether for the triangular prism.

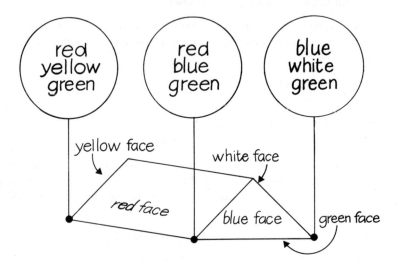

Does each colour appear the same number of times in the six sets?

Where is the red, blue, and yellow corner?

Where is red, blue, and green?

Do all the colour combinations appear at the corners?

(We leave the children's version of this question as an exercise in communication for the teacher!)

Put your finger on the edge between the red and the blue faces.

Is there only one edge like this?

11 Soup tins and tennis balls: examination of curved surfaces

We now look at cylinders and spheres. Table-tennis balls, tins, and sections of broomhandle or dowelling are suitable, given a coat of white emulsion paint or oil undercoat. The 'activity' here is mainly discussion.

Begin discussion by asking children to paint each face a different colour, as before. The queries that will inevitably follow make the young child think mathematically. How, in fact, do we define a face? Has a ball faces? Must faces be flat? If they are curved, must they end in edges? How many colours are needed to paint the faces of a cylinder?

Children given spheres and asked to paint the 'faces' will probably colour over an area roughly equivalent to their own faces. We have here a word with a mathematical use different from its ordinary use.

Introduce at this point the word 'surface' in as many ways as possible. Discuss, for example, the surface of a pond, of a table, of an egg, of a soup tin, of a sphere. Distinguish between flat and rounded or curved surfaces. Try to lead the discussion to conclusions using ordinary language, comparing spheres and cylinders with cubes and prisms.

The surface of a cube is made up with flat faces.

The surface of an egg is curved all over and has no edges.

The surface of a soup tin has two flat ends with edges, but the rest of it is rounded.

The soup tin has the same shape as the piece of broomhandle.

Ask the children to say things such as these about the shapes available.

12   Hills and valleys: the effect of shape on physical properties

This activity is one of the many relating geometrical with physical properties. Note that the geometry does not, either in terms of experience or of logic, take precedence over the material examples, but it enables them to be discussed in precise language.

Fold a card into a set of sharp ridges, as shown

If each of the slopes is numbered it allows any position along the sequence to be identified, and incidentally allows a discussion of odd and even numbers. As looked at in the diagram, only the odd numbers are visible. Why?

Ask the children to run their fingers along the card, noting that between odd and even slopes is a ridge, between even and odd is a valley, with the 'edge' underneath. Does it matter from which side we approach an edge? Let them run their fingers up and down the slopes, noting the sudden changes of direction, up to an edge, down to the next.

Now compare with a section of corrugated plastic sheet, explored also by touch, perhaps with closed eyes.

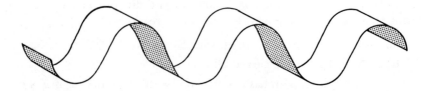

Here there are no sudden or definite changes from up to down. There are still the same ups and downs from hills to valleys, but they are gradual. There are no sharp edges.

Consolidate and extend the work by investigating the rolling of a marble on the two shapes, noting the oscillation on the corrugated surface. Marbles roll. What other shapes will roll? Let the children make a slope with a board and books, using it to sort the class collection of shapes into two groups, discussing what features they have in common.

These shapes roll: they have a rounded surface.

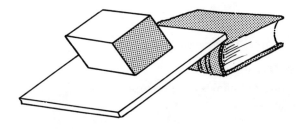

These shapes slide or topple: they have flat faces.

13 Names and things: development of vocabulary for shape

Modern packaging now provides boxes and containers in a wide range of shapes. At one time containers were only cuboids, cylinders, or the triangular prism of a well-known make of chocolate, but now square pyramids, hexagonal prisms, the tetrahedron, and other shapes are common. The names of shapes are not likely to appear in a reading scheme, but if a child is given a shape to work with as in the previous activities, there will be no difficulty about learning the name, however uncommon it may be in ordinary use.

Make a collection of shapes, preferably both actual packets and plain card or wooden models from which the shape itself emerges without the distraction of wording or design. Label them with the names written on cards. Try to keep the collection in rotation, replacing items as children bring in new examples. A common craft activity in classrooms is to make lorries, buildings, bridges, ships, road rollers, and so on from suitably shaped cartons or containers. The work can be linked with both language and mathematics if the teacher uses appropriate descriptive terms. Without thinking one says: 'Let's try the cornflakes packet and the cocoa tin.' If one has geometry in mind and one says 'We want a rectangular shape and a cylinder. Let's try . . .', the children who can follow are led into a more effective use of language.

The recognition of solid shapes from pictures in two dimensions is an acquired skill, and at first the children should be shown the solid shapes alongside the drawings of them. A work sheet will help, and can refer the pupils to the actual shapes. Note that in the example some shapes are drawn from more than one viewpoint.

Class work sheet for Activity 12.

Write in the names of these shapes.

  Some are drawn twice.

  You can find the names on the shapes table.

  One is done for you.

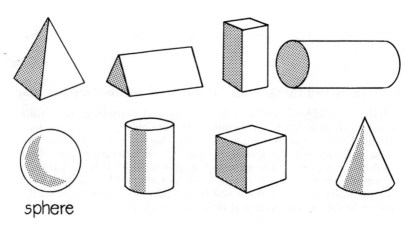

sphere

14 Drawing around shapes: a skill exercise

Drawing around given shapes is much more difficult for a small child than most adults imagine. Free drawing with a pencil is not the same as guiding it around an outline, and some children will need help in holding the pencil and keeping it in contact with the shape. It is, in fact, easier to draw round an *internal* outline, as a stencil with the shape cut out of a stiff board, because then the hand holding it down can be kept clear of the moving fingers guiding the pencil. The actual object of the exercise is to obtain circles, squares, and rectangles from the familiar solids the children have handled. The children are not yet ready to do formal constructions using instruments, but we want them to recognize and draw the figures.

Begin with a cube. Tell the child to put a face, a named face (the 'star' say), squarely onto a sheet of paper and draw round the edges. Ask what shape has been drawn, and whether it is the shape of the star face. Ask how the pencil has been moved. Would it matter which face we drew round? Children should be asked to draw their squares with the cubes stood in various ways on the paper. A square standing on one corner with a vertical diagonal may be called a diamond. We want them to grasp that a shape is a square independently of its orientation.

Now give the pupils coins, soup tins, beer mats, and other objects having circular outlines and ask them to draw round the outlines onto paper. They will, of course, draw circles of various sizes. The circles can be arranged in designs or patterns and then coloured. The key point to emerge from discussion is that all circles have exactly the same shape and differ only in size, as balls do.

Repeat the exercise using cuboid packets such as toothpaste cartons, noting that usually more than one rectangle can be drawn with each box. Discuss the word 'rectangle', which should already have been described as the shape of the side or face of the packet. It is usually necessary to take extreme examples to persuade pupils that rectangles really do have different shapes. Some of them will be slower than others to grasp the difference between the general and specific shapes already discussed in Activity 2. In any case the difference between two rectangles is less obvious than the difference between two dogs, and teachers may wish to omit this section with less able children.

As their skill develops, some children will enjoy making patterns or abstracts as in the examples shown, especially if they colour them afterwards.

They can be labelled as patterns but should have the key properties written underneath.

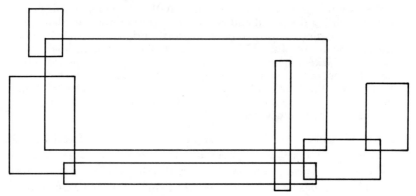

some rectangles are long and thin, others are short and fat

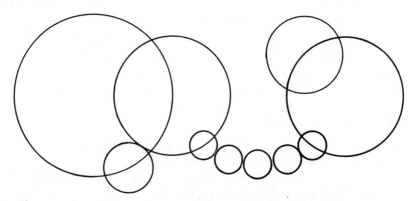

All circles have the same shape, but can have different sizes.

The child who has grasped these two facts and can discuss in what way two circles or rectangles differ is well on the way into the mathematics of spatial relations. We do not speak of these figures as 'geometrical' configurations but merely as the shapes obtained when we draw round certain common objects. The word *outline* can be used now to describe the flat shape got by drawing round an object.

An alternative starting point can be by asking a child to put a foot on a sheet of paper while another draws round it. This, of course, produces a 'footprint', commonly used in class as an arbitrary unit of measure. By analogy we are drawing the 'footprints' of objects, and can ask whether we can recognize shapes by their 'footprints'. Also ask the children to produce lists of objects having circular outlines, like plates, coins, frisbees, hoops, clock faces. Make sure that the spelling is correct in these lists. Some objects such as tin lids can be made to print their own outlines by applying paint and pressing them onto paper, or even as a direct analogy with footprints by pressing into clay.

The skill in drawing the outlines of objects and obtaining patterns from them can only come from extended activity. The child should draw round as many faces of objects as he can, preferably labelling the outlines : rectangle, triangle, square, circle. The two words 'oblong' and 'oval' may come up in discussion. These are useful words that do not have precise mathematical meanings, and are best handled in class by using them as adjectives. One would, for example, agree that the shape of a given rectangle was oblong, or that a table was oval. After (but not before) drawing some of these using boxes and containers, children can be given the plastic shapes now readily obtainable. We do not begin with these because they are 'apparatus', and not taken from the world of the children's experience. Children should try to identify and describe the shapes as they occur in or out of the classroom, and even try to draw them. The plastic shapes are useful here since they come in a range of sizes.

Here are examples of shapes in use:

15   The circle board: a first exercise in drawing circles

There is a big difference between drawing round a given circular object and actually making a circle. Small children find compasses difficult to use, and in any case this instrument does not let one *see* the radius line that is being rotated. A teacher might like to provide a circle board.

Drive a 20 mm nail from the back through the centre of a square of plywood about 10 mm thick. Round off the projecting point lightly with a file or emery cloth. A child can now put a sheet of paper on the board, pressing through it with the blunted point. Supplied with a few loops of string and a pencil, the child can now draw firm circles much more successfully than with compasses. Instead of a loop, a strip of plastic or stout card punched with small holes can be used. A device working like this is now on the market, but the improvised apparatus is more interesting to the children.

This is a very important exercise. It produces a circle as the path of the moving pencil point as it travels round the central nail at a fixed distance from it. Much later the pupil will come to a formal definition of the circle as the set of all points in a plane equidistant from a fixed point. It is through activities such as the one given that such forms of words convey intelligible concepts.

Extend the work by floating a large rubber ball in a bowl of water. Ask what is the outline of the 'hole' made in the water. Press the ball down or lift it almost clear of the water. Cut through an orange and ask the children what shape one gets on cutting through a sphere or ball.

Modify the circle board by driving in two nails 10 cm apart, so that the pencil put in a loop of string over both nails describes an ellipse. This can be drawn by a child quite unable to push in pins through a sheet of paper and manipulate a loop of thread, and many young pupils are delighted at getting such a shape so easily. There is no reason for withholding the name *ellipse* and the chances are that, having drawn it as well as having talked about it, more of a class will spell its name correctly the next day than some new word found in a reader. The children can also recognize the shape as the 'footprint' of some talcum powder containers. Here again, one uses the word 'oval' in describing a round elongated shape such as the ellipse. The concept of the ellipse as a *specific* shape is too difficult.

16 Outlines in motion: introduction to shapes in motion

Most natural shapes are not made with circles and straight lines, and it is not always easy to draw their outlines.

Get children to make outlines of their feet or of their hands spread out on a sheet of paper. (We have already mentioned the 'footprint' in Activity 13.)

Ask them to draw the outline of a potato: this is difficult unless it is cut first, drying the cut surface on a cloth, although a child can easily make a print with the potato and then draw round that. One also sees that similar potatoes give rather different outlines according to the plane in which they are cut.

A toy for very young children consists of stout wooden cut-out animals which fit into the holes from which they are cut. The animals can be used for drawing outlines very effectively. Otherwise the teacher could draw them on card and ask the children to cut them out, although stencils can always be obtained from educational suppliers. Get the child to draw the outline of the object several times on the same sheet, turning it round and round. Although a child will lack the skill to do this very well, interesting patterns can be made by turning the shape about a fixed centre, and the class might like to see such a pattern done by the teacher.

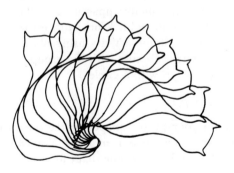

Sooner or later a child will not only turn the shape round but turn it over. If not, the teacher should see that it happens. This introduces a new and quite different kind of movement whose discussion could be difficult. It is not advisable at this stage to connect the movement with reflection of the outline in a mirror, although this will be important later.

Take an animal outline, such as an elephant, and get the child to move it along, drawing the outline several times. Now draw the outline, turn the elephant over so that it faces the other way, and draw again. The elephants are walking away from one another. Another strategy here is for the teacher to draw two outlines and ask how the elephant was moved to get them. We want the children to realize that there are three ways of moving the object before drawing the new outline which is a transformation of the first. It can be moved along (translated), turned round or twisted (rotated), and turned over (which for an outline produces the same result as reflection in a mirror). The technical terms would not of course be used in discussion with the pupils.

An extension for the more able children would be to draw the outline of one hand held open, using thin card which can afterwards be cut out. They can now draw the outline of the cut-out in the three ways, moving it along, turning it round while keeping it flat, and then turning it over. What happens to the outline of the left hand then? Those children who can follow this work should try all three movements with such shapes as they can find. Their discovery, that some shapes look exactly the same even when turned over and that others 'go in a different direction', is better left without an attempt to formulate the results. For some configurations, triangles for example, there could be a lot of confusion. They can see, nevertheless, because it is visually apparent, that the outlines of the left hands or feet transform into right. Work with mirrors will come much later, but at this stage a simple activity using plastic shapes is enough, producing 'frieze' patterns. Discuss with the group what happens if you try to make a frieze pattern with a circle.

Class work sheet for Activity 16.

Make patterns from your plastic shapes or the ones you have cut out. Draw round them and then move them along. You can twist them round or turn them over as well. Use only one shape for each pattern. Here is one done for you.

Do at least three other patterns like these with your shapes. Try to make a big pattern with the cut-out of the outline of your hand.

17 Looking at shadows: an early introduction to projection

Those who try to teach woodwork or metalwork to older but less able children know how hard it is for them to visualize the shapes of solid objects from dimensioned plans and elevations. The work which follows is an early and quite informal attempt to get children thinking about solids and their projections which will help them later. The word 'projection', of course, is not used.

Ask the children to choose a cardboard box and fasten it to a stick with drawing pins or sticky tape. Using the sun or a bright light, throw the shadow of the box onto a screen of white paper. The screen need not be vertical. Note that the shadow outline varies as the box is moved. Some of the shapes will be recognized and named, others will not.

Repeat the exercise with other shapes and discuss what happens. It is too difficult at this stage for the children actually to record the images obtained. Try also with plane shapes such as triangles, discs, and squares, noting informally what happens as they move. Many effects are striking to the eye. The shadow projection gives only the outline of the object shadowed. Faced with an actual object we recognize, we do not normally attend to the outline it presents but to the solid we know it to be. There should be no attempt to analyse or explain: all we need is to show the children that shadows can take many different shapes.

Show the children some carefully prepared drawings of objects seen from different viewpoints. Ask if the different drawings belong to the same object. Here are some examples of sets of drawings, each of which represents the same object. A few details are shown, as well as the geometric outline. These drawings are, in a technical use of the word, projections or 'shadows'. It is better not to try to link the two parts of this activity in the child's mind.

Ability to draw or even to recognize such pictures is a social or cultural skill: it took artists and craftsmen many centuries to develop the techniques of perspective and projection. The extension of this activity leads to the drawing of plans which can be introduced informally long before properly dimensioned plans can be handled. The key question is:

What would you see of this object if you looked down on it from above?

The question cannot be put on the assumption that it will be understood. One needs to ask *why* certain features appear or become invisible. If you look down on a square table from above, why do you not see the legs? If it has a drawer with a handle, why can you often see the handle? By discussion and by standing and looking down on things the child can be led to a plan of an oblong room with a few objects in it, say, a tiled hearth, a mantelshelf, a television, a few chairs, and a hearthrug with a simple pattern. A drawing can be made, using the 'footprint' of a box perhaps, to get a suitable rectangle, and labelled as the plan of a room.

18   Introduction to nets: beginning to build up solids

This is a key activity that leads eventually to the construction of solids by means of their nets (i.e., the plane shapes that give the solid figure when folded up). Here we simply give the children suitable shapes and show how the nets can be developed from them. Young children will find it hard to draw the nets accurately since the solids will slip and twist during the 'rocking over', but the attempt is a useful experience that can be recalled later when nets are studied.

It might be better to demonstrate what is to be done, and what is meant by 'rocking over'. If the children have learned the words, the instructions can now be put on to a workcard. A teacher might like to show the pupils how a net accurately drawn and cut folds up into a solid. It should be cut from thick card and heavily scored along the fold lines to bend up. This can be done before or after the children's activity.

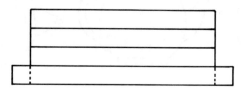

The work sheet, as given, is to be taken as a reading exercise, made up with words the children know and words to which the activity is to introduce them. It is given here in two parts, which could be done separately with different age groups.

Work sheet for Activity 18.

Ask for a die like the one in this picture.

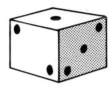

Each face is marked with dots.
Count the dots on each face.
Draw the patterns of dots and put the number under each drawing like this.
Two are done for you.

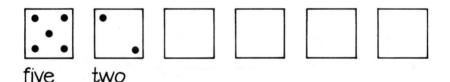

five   two

The dot patterns let you tell which face is which.

Ask for a triangular prism.
Mark each face with a dot pattern.
Lay the prism on a sheet of paper and draw round the face touching the paper.
Rock over the prism onto a different face.
If you tip it over carefully one of the edges does not move.
Draw round the new face that is on the paper.
Do all three faces and the two ends as well.
Mark each face on your drawing with the same dot patterns as on the prism.

Note:

The final net for the prism, if the triangles are equilateral, is as below, although the ends can be attached to any one of the other faces.

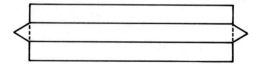

As before, one can bypass the problem of writing or reading the instructions by talk and demonstration, but this misses one of the objects of the exercise.

19 Looking at lines: opening up a simple concept

A geometrical line is an abstraction, but it is abstracted from our experience of strings, edges, paths, rods, and so on. The next activity, which could be used as a class lesson with the children (and will therefore be presented as such) begins to make this abstraction.

Draw a familiar outline on the board.

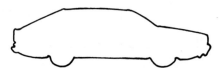

All the lines we have drawn so far have been outlines or pictures of things you know and use.

Let us draw a wavy line – any line.

Draw one in your book.

When you drew it you started somewhere and you finished somewhere.

Label the two ends – 'start' and 'finish'.

The children can be asked what such a line could represent, or even be asked to complete a picture round the line.

Waves on the sea

A whale

Draw two more lines, one curved and one straight.

Here are two paths through a dark wood.

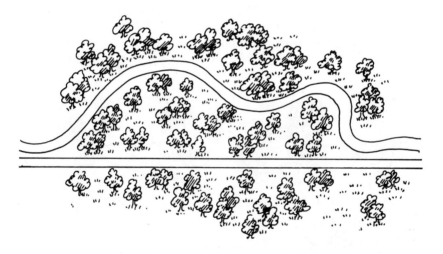

(The paths can, more convincingly, be drawn double by using two sticks of chalk held together.) One would then say:

This double line stands for a path.

On which path could you see from end to end?

The class should be able to provide the word 'straight'. The other could be 'wiggly', 'wobbly', 'twisted', or what have you: but agree in the end to call it *curved*.

Unless it is very long or there is something in the way, we can always see from end to end on a straight path. Consolidate by asking the children to draw a set of lines both curved and straight. Refer to the beginning and endings of the lines and ask them if they can imagine lines drawn so that they go on 'for ever', or at least out of sight.

20 Paths and points

This is a straightforward activity that investigates the shortest path between two points. To be effective the children should use as large a sheet of paper as possible, so that the difference in lengths of the strings or tapes is easily seen.

The sheet of paper represents the sea. The children should draw an island on the sheet as large as possible, trying to make it look like an island. It could also be coloured. Draw two houses on the island, one at each end, and then, using cut string, thread or tape, lay down three possible paths from one house to the other. Each string should start at one house and finish at the other.

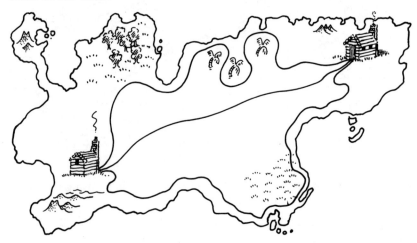

Crayon along the paths laid down and remove the strings. Hang up the strings, or hold them up by one end, to see which is the shortest and which the longest. Not many groups are likely to have made one of the paths straight, but the discussion can go ahead.

You have drawn lines to represent paths.

The paths you have made have different shapes, and some are longer than others.

If you haven't got one, draw in a straight path; that is, you draw a straight line between the houses.

Which of the paths would you take if you were in a hurry?

Think of some reasons for having more than one path.

The conclusions to be reached are such as these:

Straight lines do not change direction.

The shortest path between two places is straight.

Most lines have beginnings and endings, although we can imagine lines going on and on.

Curved lines can make many shapes.

Extend, by introducing the word 'point' as a name given to the start or finish of a line. Say that we can show a point with a dot. Ask the children to make two dots and draw a line between them. Also discuss whether a straight line has a 'shape'. Conclude that it has, since one can pick it out by its shape from a set of other lines. Ask the children to mark two points on a sheet of paper and then join them by lines.

The word 'point' has several distinct uses, and we refer to this difficulty (this point) in Activity 25.

21 Closed and open curves: some more properties of lines

This extends the earlier work by discussing *closure*.

Somes lines cross themselves, once or several times.

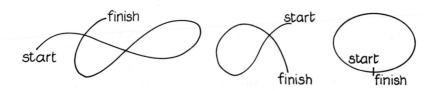

Does the third line cross itself? No, but it ends where it began. We say that it is *closed*. It encloses a shape. The other lines that cross also, for part of their length, enclose shapes. They could all be fences. Draw one.

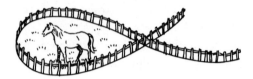

Where would it be safe to keep a horse?
Some lines are closed: they shut in a space.

Some shapes are open.

Some are both.

Get the children to draw examples of each and label them. Some may have difficulty in accepting that a simple straight line is 'open', in the sense that we are using the word, and the matter should be discussed. A closed curve or closed portion of a curve could be the shape of a fence to shut in a plot of land. An open fence cannot enclose a space, and could not keep in animals (or keep out children).

Extend the use of the word 'point'. It not only applies to the start and finish of lines, but to any position along them. If two lines cross they cross at a point. Get the children to draw some lines which cross (or join), and ask them to mark the end points and crossing points with heavier dots.

22 Lines as paths: lines that tell us where to go

We want children to get used to lines which represent paths in diagrams which contain other lines which do not represent paths. A good exercise uses a map to mark a journey. A first attempt should be made on a large-scale map of the area surrounding the school (scale 1:2500), mounted on a thick card and preferably covered with adhesive film.

Pin a sheet of tracing paper over the map placed on a horizontal surface. Discuss the location of marked features relative to the school, then allow children to use coloured fibre tip pens to mark in routes between them. Choose the routes so that they do not all start from the school; otherwise it soon becomes necessary to renew the paper. When pupils are used to this activity they can use a plan of an unfamiliar or imaginary locality on which a suitable route is marked.

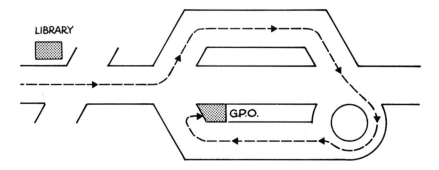

The children can be asked to imagine themselves driving a car from the library to the post office along the route shown by a dotted line, and to point out the places at which they turn left, right, or stop. They can be asked to trace in the shortest route and to give possible reasons for the one actually taken. There are explanations other than one-way streets. An able group could, alone or with help, write out the instructions for the journey. Many quite young children know that lines marked on the road have meanings for motorists. Some road safety posters show important road markings, and are likely to be available in schools. Lines on roads convey information or give instructions, and this should be discussed with the children. Quite young children will know that a broken line marks the middle of the road, and that a continuous white one should not be crossed by a car. They should, of course, be aware of zebra crossings, and it is worth while to note how these and their approaches are marked out with lines and shapes.

Note that the activity as given assumes that the children are used to being in cars. In an inner-city school, or certainly in a deprived area, this would not be true. The proposed journey should then be on foot, again with discussion of the detour, in a plan suitably modified.

23 Looking at straight lines: a closer look at one kind of line

We hope that the geometrical line is now beginning to emerge as a concept, but we must still refer it to concrete examples.

Make sure that the children concerned can use rulers to draw straight lines. This is a skill that needs teaching. The fingers and thumb should be opened as far as possible and used to press down the ruler, preferably spanning the part of the ruler to be used. Otherwise the ruler twists under the fairly heavy sideways pressure that young children seem to apply when keeping the point of the pencil in contact.

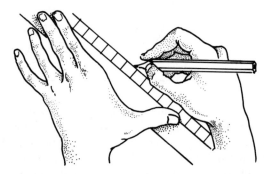

Let the children draw pairs of lines that meet, join, or cross, putting a heavy dot where they touch. The word 'point' can be used again here: the dot marks the point where the lines meet. The diagrams look much better when the dots are large, and these should be drawn with a small circular movement of the pencil, not merely by pressing it hard. Most later diagrams will be drawn without the dots, but we are now discussing both points and lines and need to represent them.

The demand for a pair of lines that does not meet will most likely produce a diagram such as

and open up a profitable discussion about what would happen if we made one line or both a little longer. Eventually we get the pair

which can be extended indefinitely (as mentioned in Activities 19 and 20) without meeting. Examples such as railway lines can be discussed. The word *parallel* can now be given in context, and the more able children can be asked whether they think the opposite sides of rectangles or the opposite edges of rulers are in fact parallel. Can a rectangular card be used to draw a pair of parallel lines?

24   This way, please: the concept of direction

Here we introduce the straight line as an indicator of direction. Most children will have used this word in conversation, in phrases such as 'go off in the wrong direction', and we now have the opportunity to use it more precisely. The topic can make a group or class lesson since it does not depend on reading ability.

Draw some straight lines on a blackboard. As each one is drawn use a statement such as 'Let's start here and draw the chalk in this direction.'

Do the lines mark directions unambiguously? To get the point home it will probably be necessary to draw, very deliberately, a pair of parallel lines, one from right to left and the other from left to right. To make the direction clear an arrow is needed: the suggestion may come from somebody in the class.

We conclude that a line with an arrow on it marks a direction.

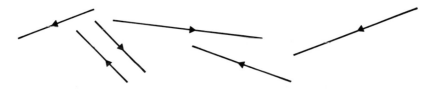

There are always two ways of moving along a line.

This work needs to be consolidated and extended in as many ways as possible. Each illustration, as the examples show, can be a valuable piece of work in its own right, each linking up the formal concept with a real situation.

Use the large-scale map and the tracing paper to mark a pupil's route both to and from school.

Make drawings of road signs that use arrows. These can include arrows that show change of direction, like the 'right turn' sign.

Use a plan as produced in Activity 17.

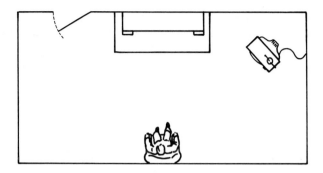

Mark on the plan (or on a piece of tracing paper placed over it) lines that show the direction in which the girl has to look to see the fire, the door, the TV set.

Another approach to the use of the plan, best given at this stage without comment as a 'throwaway' demonstration, is to pin a piece of tracing paper over the girl's head in the plan so that it can be rotated. A line drawn from the pin to the edge of the paper can then be directed in turn to the various objects shown in the room, and represents her line of sight.

25 Sharp points and blunt points: an early introduction to angles

In Activity 22 we marked the meeting points of lines with a dot, to mark this property of concurrence. Here the dot is omitted to draw attention to the shape produced.

Draw pairs of lines that make sharp points and blunt points.

Among the several uses of the word point is that of the meeting place of two lines and also the actual shape we think of as 'pointed'. It is better to clear up this ambiguity by using the words in suitable contexts.

Get the children to draw pairs of lines and name them as they think fit. It is better not to introduce the technical words 'acute' and 'obtuse', whose meaning is discussed in Activity 33. The same exercise, with one of the lines horizontal, gives us the word 'slope'. We can without actually using the word 'horizontal' say that some lines which meet form (or look like) slopes. Slopes are either steep or gentle. Imagine a car running down them.

Consolidate the work by using strips of card or lath jointed at the ends.

The strips can be held and opened to produce sharp or blunt points, steep or gentle slopes. With able pupils the word 'angle' can be informally introduced: a sharp point has a small angle, a blunt point a larger one.

26 Steep slopes and gentle slopes: the concept of stability

The use of the word 'slope' allows a discussion of balance. As with many of these activities, the full implications must be kept till greater insight is possible, but this is an important concept and needs to be made clear. The work is related to Activity 12.

Balance a pencil on a flat hardcover book placed on the table. Now open the book to make a slope and try again. Children enjoy lifting the cover very carefully to see what slope can be made before the pencil topples. Repeat with an upright cylindrical shape of greater radius, such as a sweet tube, and then with a glass marble or a large ball bearing. A good discussion can arise by asking how we can tell if a surface is level. Can a smooth marble help us find out? It is clear that some shapes balance on slopes more easily than others, and some begin to slide before they show signs of toppling. The special case of rolling and its relation to toppling is too difficult for discussion, but can be left simply as the observation that spheres and cylinders roll down slopes.

Relate conclusions to practical considerations by asking suitable questions.

Why do roofs have slopes?
What would happen if the floor of this room were a steep slope?
Why is a steep hill marked with a warning sign for motorists?
What happens if you play ball on a hill?
Why do rivers run into the sea?

27 The triangle as a shape: an important configuration

This is another topic which, if apparatus is made in advance, can be given as a class lesson. Commercially supplied strips and fasteners are available.

Punch rows of holes evenly down each side of strips of card of various widths, then guillotine them between the holes to make 'geo-strips' of different lengths.

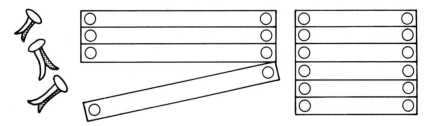

Give each pupil a set of three strips and paper fasteners so that between them members of the class will make equilateral, isosceles, and scalene triangles with both acute and obtuse angles. Make sure that a few pupils get two short strips whose total length is less than that of the third. Discuss the shapes formed.

At this stage only the words 'triangle' and 'equilateral triangle' need be learned, but the various configurations can be described informally. It is well worth while getting the children to formulate, from the 'failure set' of strips, the conditions under which three lengths will form a triangle. If the strips are cut to whole numbers of centimetres they can be measured and the results will give useful practice in mental addition and subtraction.

The triangles can be classified according to the way they are made up, and there is plenty of scope for mounting them on wall displays.

For example, a set of triangles

    using three equal strips
    using two equal strips, the third different
    using three unequal strips
    having a blunt corner
    having all corners sharp

This exercise avoids the technical words *isosceles* and *scalene*.

Plastic, wood, or gummed paper shapes should also be available. The children can be asked to compare these with the shapes formed by the strips, and to draw their outlines.

Extend the work by abstracting from the strips two configurations of three straight lines drawn on paper.

The equilateral triangle can also be produced by paper folding, using a cut-out circular shape made with the circle board of Activity 15.

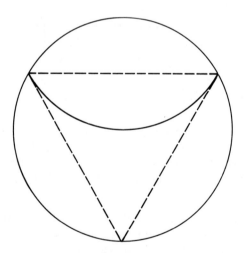

Fold the edge of the circular shape to touch the central hole. Fold in the edge again from the end of the previous fold. The third fold completes the triangle.

A triangle of base 8 units and height 7, although not exactly equilateral, is equal sided within the limits of ordinary measurement (the base angle is only ¼° out). Given a square grid, mark out a line 8 units long and from its mid-point count up 7 units to find the vertex. Children may find it easier to use 'dotty paper', printed with dots in square arrays, rather than the usual squared graph paper.

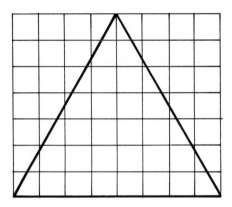

This is a convenient way of marking out triangles which are equilateral for all classroom purposes. With much older children the failure of the construction to give an exact figure can usefully lead to a more mathematical discussion, but this is a sixth-form topic.

A novel alternative approach, which can be done as revision at a later date, is to provide pupils with sets of *four* sticks or milk straws, cut to appropriate lengths. The assignment is to make as many different triangles as possible by putting together, on a sheet of paper, the four sticks in sets of three. As each triangle is made, its corners can be marked by dots which are afterwards joined up with a ruler and pencil.

28 Putting a straight line to use: the beginnings of geometry in action

Here we talk about some of the uses to which we can put a single straight line. There are many others, more than we can usefully discuss with the age range.

The work is suitable for both class and group discussion, perhaps with the teacher recording or illustrating on the board. The question is simply: where can we use a straight line and what do we use it for? Here are some examples:

All children are asked to bring their

dinner money on <u>Tuesday</u>, not Monday.

composer. He was born in ~~1789~~ 1798. He wrote many famous operas. The Barber of Seville is the most famous of all

✧ *Sweets* ✧

apple pie and Cream

~~Ice cream~~

Blackcurrant tart

It can be used to underline something important which must be noted, to delete a mistake, or to tell us that an item on a list is no longer available.

Discuss examples with the children.

In these examples, it is not the line itself, but *where* it is that gives it its meaning.

A broken straight line has more than one meaning as a road marking : it can mark the middle or the side of a road, or the edge of a traffic lane. Once again its position is important, but here the broken form of the line tells us that it may be crossed by a vehicle if it is safe to do so. A short straight line is used with numbers to mean subtract, 10 − 6 means 'ten subtract six'.

Straight lines are often used with an arrow to show direction: left, right, or straight ahead. The children can suggest examples.

 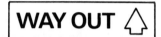 

The Highway Code will give others, and also shows that lines as drawn can be distinguished by colour − not normally something that concerns geometry.

With help, probably from leading questions, able children might eventually see the three basic properties of a straight line that enable us to use it in these ways. A straight line has

Position

Direction

Length

Of these, direction is ambiguous and needs to be fixed by an arrow, but length has so far only arisen incidentally in that we use long or short lines. Although this book presents geometry as a largely qualitative study, it is clear that work in measure can be combined with many of the activities presented, and many teachers would wish to do this. Activity 27 is another example of an opportunity for incidental work in number and measure.

29 The direction board: a practical use for lines

This is a project based on the directional concepts developed in Activity 24, as used on the topographic plates sometimes set up on hill tops that command a good view. Although the wooden stand may be left up permanently, if there is room for it, it should be clear that the construction of lines should be redrawn as often as it is needed.

Although not all schools have views of distant mountains and some playgrounds are behind high walls, one must surely be able to see something, if only a factory chimney, a tall lamp post, or a block of flats. A wooden table set up in a school corridor could serve, or a more fortunately sited school could arrange for a level board on a stout post in a corner of the playing field.

Set up a 10 cm vertical rod the thickness of a pencil near the edge of the table or board. A permanent board could have a hole drilled near its edge to take a length of dowel rod.

Fix a large sheet of paper to the table with its edge touching the dowel rod. Children working in pairs now take turns, one of them holding a second sighting rod, fixing the directions of such features as they can see and marking them as lines on the paper. Each line is labelled with the name of the feature, and each pair of children produces its own sighting sheet. It may be necessary to show the children how to sight with the two rods.

One would not expect great accuracy from this exercise. A teacher would need to check the possibilities in the light of the actual school, its position and its outlook. The point of it is that it puts lines to use.

30 Putting two straight lines to use: lines that give instructions

Here we discuss possible uses of a pair of straight lines. Most of these give a *picture* of an actual situation.

The lists of standard traffic signs in the Highway Code show many examples. It is important that children should give or be given the current signs, although of course many older forms are still seen on the roads. The 'picture' aspect of many of the signs is clear.

The double parallel white lines on the road, like the 'equals' sign in arithmetic, is an example of a conventional use: they are not pictures but symbols. The best classroom strategy for this activity is probably demonstration of two or three uses, leaving children to gather others, perhaps over a weekend. Its value as an exercise in the Highway Code – in effect a cross-classification of the signs using their shape – is obvious. Because of this aspect of the work, it is also advisable to collect the two-line signs in two stages, omitting at first those with arrows linking them to directions. This also provides an opportunity for the introductory question given the day before, so often valuable with younger children.

Some of the two straight-line signs in the Highway Code have arrows. How many do? Try to find out.

The classification can also be extended, as long as we make clear to the children that we are now relaxing one of our conditions, to include two lines which are not straight, as in the 'road narrows' sign.

An earlier Activity 22 has already tacitly introduced a curved direction line, and we can now go back to the work of Activity 26 and extend our collection of single lines to curves or direction changes.

Once again we have an activity that might need to be modified for an inner-city area, but surely all children should know as much as possible about the Highway Code.

31   Looking at geoboards: an introduction to the apparatus

Although the geoboard (or nailboard) is one of the most generally useful of all pieces of apparatus for introducing geometry, children need to get used to using it. At this stage it is better to continue exercises which help to make the boards familiar, which practise following verbal instructions and which keep in use the vocabulary of direction and position. What follows consolidates the work of the previous activity.

Using 9-pin geoboards – the most useful size – get the pupils to obey instructions given verbally. This in itself is a useful group or class exercise, as long as there is one board for each child. Typical instructions would be:

Stretch a band right across the top and another across the bottom of the board. Now take the bands off and put them on again so that they go up and down at each side.

Now put the bands from corner to corner.

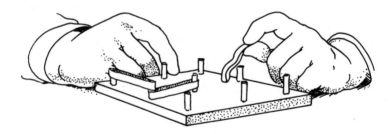

The word *diagonally* can be introduced as a synonym for 'from corner to corner' in this context. The work is best done with groups small enough for the teacher to keep an eye on individuals in order to spot those who have difficulties or have to wait for their neighbours. If a bright child obeys the second instruction by simply twisting the board through 90°, the teacher has the option of opening up a discussion at a higher level, perhaps by asking why the bands were not taken off. A good follow-up question would be:

If I had not been watching, would I have known whether Tim took the bands off or not?

Such a discussion should be kept informal: it can be allowed to develop if the pupils continue it, but should not with this age group be developed by the teacher. The geoboard has its most interesting uses with older children, but the opportunity of introducing it should be taken early.

Consolidate by asking the children to make up patterns with coloured bands according to instructions.

Put green bands across the top and bottom, blue bands up and down the sides, and white bands diagonally.

A geoboard pattern in coloured chalk can be drawn on a blackboard and a description asked for, or children can work for a while in pairs, each making a pattern that the other describes. The work can also be extended by asking the children to copy their patterns on suitable paper, on duplicated sheets set out with patterns of nine dots representing the nails on the board.

It is also possible to give the instructions on written workcards, which then become good exercises in reading instructions. A written version of the above could become:

Put green bands right across the top and bottom of your geoboard, blue bands up and down the two sides, and white bands diagonally from corner to corner. Then draw in your book the shape you have made.

32   Another look at cubes: continuing a detailed examination

Whenever two lines meet they form an angle, but when talking of paths or streets we usually use the word corner. We have already classified corners as blunt or sharp. We are now going to consider the corners or angles of each face of a cube as distinct from its eight vertices. This carries on the detailed examination of the cube begun in Activity 8, where the word 'corner' was used in the way most children would use it. We shall here introduce them to the word 'vertex'. This work is more suitable for a small group, who can sit with the teacher round a table.

Refer back to the earlier set of activities, where we identified faces, edges, and vertices of a cube by colour or the use of a motif. Check that pupils use the word 'edge' here to mean the line along which any pair of faces of the cube meet. Check their number, preferably by reference to one of the original marked cubes.

Now have a large cardboard cube with its faces marked with motifs as before, but with each of its twelve edges coloured. A thin strip of coloured gummed paper along each edge is excellent for the purpose, and reinforces the cube. We have now a quite unambiguous way of referring to each of the eight faces of the cube, simply by naming the colours that enclose them.

We can also ask questions which, calling for sound mathematical insight, can nevertheless be answered by observation and handling the cube. The answers may not be immediately obvious to the teacher who asks them, which perhaps establishes the credentials of the questions to be mathematics.

For example:

Do we need to colour *every* edge to name the faces?

Discussion: since two faces share an edge, one edge alone does not define a face, but any two of the four colours will do so. Referring to the diagram – the children, of course, should be referred to the actual cube – we can see that the star face is also labelled as red/green and the moon face as blue/yellow. The broken lines represent the various colours.

Labelling each of the remaining edges of the top and bottom faces, now let us name all the faces, so we have done the job with eight colours.

We can name each face of the cube with eight coloured edges.

Can we do it with less?

Is the answer obvious? In fact, it can be done with six, labelling the three edges that meet at any pair of diagonally opposite vertices. Have a cube prepared with six coloured edges to show this. Children will be able to check, by choosing any face, that the six colours suffice to name it.

Now discuss the corners, allowing the ambiguity to emerge during the discussion. By corner do we mean the point where the red, black, and blue edges meet, or the corner of the star face where the two edges red and black meet? Hence introduce the word 'vertex' – and its plural 'vertices' – in context. A vertex of a cube is where three of its edges meet : the other feature we shall continue to call the 'corner of one of the faces', although the word 'angle' can be used if preferred. We shall leave the problem of deciding the minimum number of coloured edges needed to name all the vertices, remarking that it can be done by examining the cube and that the minimum number can be arranged in several ways.

The children will see that all twelve colours are needed if we are to designate each of the four corners of each of the six faces. The twelve colours appear in a pattern of combinations as pairs for each of the twenty-four corners, but any consideration of this is beyond the children. Once again, we do not investigate all the possible questions that arise, although we might reasonably ask how many corners have a given colour in their designation.

Note that the use of the words 'vertex' and 'corner' are not precisely distinguished. Someone who insists on referring to the 'vertices' of a hexagon would certainly also refer to the 'corners' of a hexagonal tile if actually using it. Although, in general, one should avoid a technical term if an ordinary word is available, the end in view is still in using all appropriate language. Common sense is the only guide.

33 Angles: extending the concept

Although we need not have done so, we have referred only to lines which make points and corners, deferring the word 'angle'. It is hoped that the use of the word at this stage will serve to revise and extend the concept, and make it possible to classify angles.

The most effective piece of apparatus here is made from two laths pivoted together at one end, preferably fastened with a thumb screw that can be easily tightened to set them at a given angle. Refer to the earlier work on sharp and blunt points or corners formed by lines, and introduce the word 'angle' as formed when two lines go off in different directions. The words 'acute' and 'obtuse' can be demonstrated and taken for our purpose as equivalent to sharp and blunt.

Move the arms from obviously acute to obviously obtuse a few times, then stop at 90°. This angle can be compared with that at the corners of squares and rectangles, and given the name *right angle*, taken as equivalent to 'square corner'. The children could be asked both to draw, with rulers, a few examples of pairs of lines forming acute, obtuse, and right angles, and to form them on geoboards or with geo-strips and paper fasteners.

The concept of angle, especially later when we come to associate it with measure, is a difficult one, and from now on the word needs to be used in as many contexts as possible. Get the children to make angle indicators by drawing and cutting out two equal circles on the circle board, one on coloured and one on white stiff paper. Draw a radius from centre to circumference of each and cut along the line.

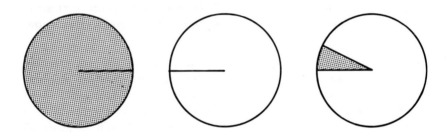

The two discs can now be slotted together so that one rotates in the other, exposing a coloured angle which can be adjusted continuously.

Using both this indicator and the pivoted laths, form an angle of 180°. Children may reasonably deny that this is an angle, but by moving the arms continuously from a very small acute angle to a large obtuse angle they may be persuaded that the arms still form an angle even when opened a little more. Give the name *straight angle*. The large dot is useful here in drawing acute, obtuse, and straight angles, since it shows the pivot or centre of rotation.

All teachers are familiar with the right angle produced by two folds in a scrap of paper. Children can form them and hold them in a large paper fastener to make 'angle testers', using them to show that the angles at the corner of doors, windows, sheets of paper, and the like are all equal and correspond to the folded paper.

We do not recommend that young children should work with zero or reflex angles. Obviously such matters raised by pupils are dealt with as they arise at the teacher's discretion. The four terms, acute, obtuse, right, and straight angles, are quite enough for nine-year-olds to learn to use with confidence.

34   A look at surfaces: the words 'horizontal' and 'vertical'

We have already used or drawn attention to surfaces such as the face of a cube or the roof, but not explicitly, and this activity is concerned with them. Earlier work suggested testing slopes by means of a rolling marble or cylinder, and we now take this up again, introducing the words 'horizontal' and 'vertical'.

Remind children of, and get them to repeat, the earlier work in which they tested for slopes using a marble. A large glass marble is satisfactory but a really large ball bearing is better. We now say that a surface such as the flat top of a table, on which a sphere will not roll wherever it is placed, is *horizontal*. Children can test available surfaces, and make lists of those that are not horizontal, but sloping. Because of the importance of tabulated information, it is worth while getting older children to draw up a neat table, ruling up the necessary lines on feint squared paper.

HORIZONTAL	SLOPING
Table	Window sill
Floor	Ramp

Ask whether *all* horizontal surfaces can be tested with a marble and discuss the less simple cases. Is the ceiling horizontal, or the surface of a pond or a bowl of water?

The word *vertical* is less easy. The teacher can make a plumb line and demonstrate its use against a door frame, then ask the children to make their own. They will probably have difficulty with the plumb line, since the cord needs to be held away from the wall to allow for the width of the bob. Fastening the cord to the centre of a block of wood helps. Some will enjoy fastening a weight by a thread to the end of a stout rod and using the device to 'fish for angles'. By holding it up to pivoted windows and the like the angle can be seen as a deviation from the vertical.

It is probably better to avoid all reference to measure in degrees at this stage. Children should, however, learn to use the two words horizontal and vertical. A table top may look horizontal, but the use of a ball shows it to be sloping. It is worth while to raise two legs of a solid large table very slightly, say, by resting each on a centimetre cube. The ball will roll on this surface, and a length of dowelling cut off carefully square will topple, even though it can be balanced on a true horizontal.

Once the two words horizontal and vertical are grasped they can be used to describe horizontal and vertical lines. Refer to Activities 25 and 26.

35 Evaluation (ii)

Since this early work in geometry has little in common with learning number facts or processes in arithmetic, there are no standardized tests that can be applied and we feel that they would be inappropriate even if available. What concerns us is that the child's developing skills in handling material and using language should include and in turn be helped by reference to geometric concepts. Evaluation then takes the form of noting progress as it takes place, but it often pays to take stock by presenting children with a prepared set of questions and tasks designed to test understanding. It remains an individual matter between child and teacher.

Give the following questions or instructions to the children, wording them to suit the circumstances of the class. There will be some children for whom the questions as written are suitable.

How would you draw a line on a notice so that it shows you in which direction to go?

Draw me an obtuse angle.

Make a right angle using this piece of paper.

What is the name we give to an angle that is more pointed than a right angle?

Pick out from this collection of shapes a triangular prism, a cylinder, a . . .

Draw the outline (the 'footprint') of the end of the cylinder on this sheet of paper.

Mark any three dots on this sheet of paper and use your ruler to draw a triangle with the dots at the corners.

How many edges, faces, and vertices has this solid?

Use the plumb line to show me something in the room that is not vertical.

Draw an ellipse (oval) using the circle board with two nails, and cut it out carefully.

Draw the outline of this shape. Move it and draw it again.

Turn it round and draw. Turn it over and draw.

Make three *different* triangles with this set of sticks.

There is no new exercise here. We are trying to satisfy ourselves that the pupil has made progress in skill and understanding. One can, of course, extend the activities by making them more searching. For example, the child can be asked to count the faces, vertices, and edges on a solid – a hexagonal pyramid say – that he has not met before, or to join up four points with a ruler in all six possible ways, extending the lines beyond the points.

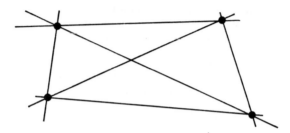

We are not concerned with the mathematical structure of this configuration, but only the child's skill in drawing it accurately. It is worth noting that, although we are now evaluating a wider range of skills and knowledge, the exercises given do not call for general concepts such as 'sameness' as does the earlier Activity 6.

36   Putting three straight lines to use: how lines help us to write

As the number of lines increases the range of uses extends: the amount of information that can be put across by their configurations increases. Beyond three or four, however, we do not normally make the analysis into lines – except for special configuration such as octagons which are of geometrical interest.

Ask children to draw sets of three straight lines. In a class lesson these can be collected and compared with discussion of the different arrangements. *Examples:*

The use of the words 'same' and 'different' in this situation can be discussed. The figures drawn by the children would probably be all different in the sense that no two are alike, but clearly they can be classified according to chosen criteria of 'sameness': some, for example, will be triangles. The last of the configurations given above is interesting. Is it a triangle, or does it only become one if we rub out the extra bits of line? A mathematician would certainly call it a triangle, but at this stage it is an opportunity to talk about words.

Discuss which road signs are made with three straight lines. Collect letters, numbers, and mathematical or other signs made up of one, two, or three straight lines.

$$I-/+=LT7XVAN4FEZYHK$$

Bright nine-year-olds will usually be delighted with a few letters from the Greek alphabet or even the Runic 'futhark' in which the first Old English and Norse inscriptions were written. The teacher, of course, must either know them or be prepared to look them up and provide enough background to put them in a context.

Γ gamma Δ delta Λ lambda Π pi

ᚠ ᛏ ᚹ ᛃ ᛗ ᛊ ᚤ ᛁ
f t w y m z k i

The Runic letters are largely made up with straight lines because they were commonly cut or scratched deeply into wood or stone, and it is easier to cut straight lines than curves. This is an example of 'applied geometry'.

Children can also try four-line letters like W or M. Bright children may be interested in the early Irish Ogham characters, which in one form are simply straight lines scratched across a long vertical or horizontal line.

t   o   r   b

They might also like to know that the basic Chinese characters are classified by the number of strokes they contain. The strokes are sometimes shown as straight lines in a modern script.

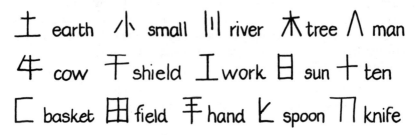

If the children copy them they should write the English equivalents neatly beside them as shown. We do not think children will gain much insight by going beyond four lines except as patterns, and they are too young to consider the intersections and bounded regions made up of lines in general. This is best regarded as a treat to come, and can be seen in the light of our comment on page 27. The next activity deals with a special case.

37 The four-line configuration: a glimpse of more formal geometry

The teacher will have to make a decision at this point. Configurations of four lines include all the quadrilaterals with special properties: the parallelograms, trapeziums, rhombuses, and so on studied on an ordinary school geometry course. Much of this work is inappropriate, not only for nine-year-olds, but for the less able children in later age groups. These are unlikely to respond to the information that rectangles are necessarily parallelograms but parallelograms not necessarily rectangles! It is often good tactics in a classroom to tell a child who seems interested that more will be done next year, as long as the teacher knows that it will be.

Refer to the square and the rectangle as now-familiar shapes made up with four straight lines, and let the children work with geoboards or draw other quadrilaterals, by joining up sets of four points on a sheet of paper using ruled lines or by drawing round solids that have faces other than rectangles. Such shapes are now quite common in modern packaging. The decision to name these configurations can be taken in the circumstances of the class but a fuller discussion of properties should be delayed, together with classification into sets by means of these properties.

The key activity is to make up some four-sided figures using punched strips and paper fasteners as in Activity 27. How do the shapes formed differ from triangles? Children will soon see that the three-strip is a fixed shape, the four-strip flexible. This is sometimes expressed by saying that the triangle is 'rigid', but if made with cardboard or plastic strips this is hardly the best word. Ask the children to record by drawing some of the shapes they can get from a given four-strip by moving it. Some of them will get quadrilaterals with re-entrant angles or even intersecting sides, as in the diagram.

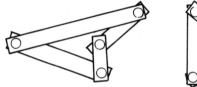 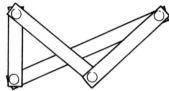

These should be included with the others, remarking how they differ.

The work can be extended by the able pupils by putting a strut across the four-strip and noting that it now forms two triangles and becomes incapable of movement. The process can be repeated for five or even six strips, but the children are unlikely to be ready for further investigation. The importance of the exercise for geometry is not simply that the four-strip configuration moves, but that later one will want to discuss the nature of the movement, particularly when one of the strips is fixed. The steering geometry of a car depends on the properties of a linkage of this type. It is of course true that the triangle is often seen as a strut or tie-rod supporting a shelf or bracket or in the structure of older railway bridges; but any steel-frame building or box-girder span in course of erection shows that the appeal to the structural uses of the properties of triangles as a motive for teaching them is somewhat misplaced. Few practical load-bearing structures are made of rods freely jointed.

A parallel exercise gets the children to form the shapes under discussion on geoboards. Teachers will find it interesting to compare what is found out about the shapes by using the two methods. The elastic bands, unlike the strips, can be stretched, but the geoboard does not allow flexible joints.

38 Beyond the quadrilateral: more names for shapes

What follows is given as an exercise in nomenclature, in the use of language rather than in the study of structure.

Refer to and if necessary extend the collection of triangular, square, hexagonal, or other plane shapes – beer mats, biscuit packet labels, cartons, and the like which should be sorted into sets according to number of sides. With these, and with commercially produced plastic shapes, let the children draw the outlines of the common polygons. Most of these will be regular, since the others rarely appear in manufactured objects. These can be drawn on paper and coloured, or drawn on coloured gummed paper, cut out and stuck on wall charts. They should be discussed as a series of shapes characterized by the number of sides they possess, and those whose sides and angles are equal should be selected for particular attention. These are the regular polygons. At this stage one only wants the children to recognize and name a few of them:

equilateral triangle

square

regular pentagon

regular hexagon

regular octagon

The rhombus can be included as it is commonly found in sets of shapes.

The children can be asked to count the sides of a fifty pence coin, and can be given the name heptagon, but here the shape is not made with straight lines. The reason for the odd choice of shape is interesting but beyond the grasp of the children : it allows the coin to be distinguished by touch yet, because it has a constant height when rolled on its edge, it can be used in slot machines. It is one more example of geometry in action. The figures can also be set up and identified using geoboards, which allow irregular polygons but not (apart from the square) the regular ones.

Small regular polygons cut from coloured gummed paper can be bought from educational suppliers. If available in quantity ask the children to build up pictures with one shape that can be labelled, for example:

My triangle man

My hexagon animal

Monster with squares

This work is a valuable preliminary to tessellation and work with area at a later stage. Children can easily make up equal-sided polygons from punched strips and paper fasteners, but since the angles are not fixed there is not much they can do with them except strut them. An 'enrichment' activity which most children enjoy is to fasten all available strips together end to end and then join the ends. The children can now all stand in a circle round their many-sided figure, keeping it in shape. They will probably call the resulting polygon a circle, and there is no harm in this, although the wise teacher will add 'not exactly'.

39 Straight lines in three dimensions: solids bounded by lines in space

It would be a pity to leave the making of shapes with straight lines without some work in three dimensions, but we shall restrict the work to very simple configurations.

Milk straws and pipe cleaners are quite satisfactory for this work, although various commercial kits are available which do the job more elegantly. Cut up some of the pipe cleaners into shorter lengths determined by previous trial. The cleaner fits better if doubled, and is most effective if bent into 3 or 4 points as shown:

When the models are made satisfactorily it is better to ask the children to take them to pieces again and reassemble them after dipping the pipe cleaners in glue. They then form surprisingly rigid skeleton shapes. Begin by making a demonstration model to show what is wanted. The easiest shape is the tetrahedron, and children like both making and naming this.

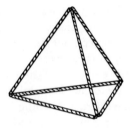

Ask the children to make a shape like the roof of a house, using straws cut to length. The exercise shows how complicated shapes are built up.

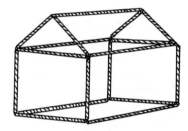

Note that when made into plane polygons the configurations are no more flexible than triangles, because the pipe cleaners do not allow rotation at the joints. The figures always seem reluctant to lie flat if they are anything other than triangles.

40   Patterns with plane shapes: designs by movement

Earlier we spoke of building up patterns from simple plane shapes. We now have more shapes available and a vocabulary to discuss what is being done. The children continue to make patterns, but the emphasis is more on describing than making them.

Supply pupils with cut-out shapes in gummed paper or issue plastic shapes whose outlines can be drawn and coloured. Note that the two kinds of apparatus need not produce the same results, since the plastic shapes can always be turned over whereas the gummed shapes can only be used one way up. It is better to do the first work with gummed paper shapes commercially supplied as an introduction to the activity, keeping the plastic shapes till later when the pupils can handle them. Pupils often fail to see that a shape has been turned over till the difference is pointed out. Whenever a pattern has been made the child should be asked to say how it has been made up: unless this is done the activity becomes trivial.

Here are some examples of frieze patterns and the sort of language that might emerge. We include the 'turn over' operation.

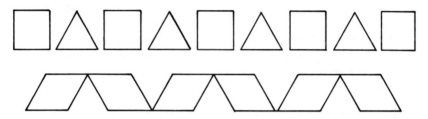

The child is asked to describe these patterns in ordinary language; one must avoid the premature introduction of technical terms such as 'translation' even if they happen to be known to the teacher. Typical phrases which should be looked for could be:

> followed by
>
> turned round
>
> turned over
>
> moved along

Few children will find it easy to give precise and accurate descriptions of the patterns, even in ordinary language. Some will find it very difficult and clearly the teacher needs to decide what help should be given.

41 Looking at cuboid boxes: how shapes are made

A once typical approach to solid shapes in geometry was via the 'net', already described in Activity 18 as the array of plane shapes that would fold up into a hollow solid, as a cube can be formed of six squares hinged together. This is one more example of the two-dimensional viewpoint forced on the world of solid objects by diagrams and the written word. The word 'net' is itself suspect since it obviously refers to the diagram of squares, and not the pieces of card or wood, which could be glued together directly. Our own suggested approach to the study of solid objects is already given in Activity 17.

Nevertheless, very many of the 3D objects that we use in the home are containers or boxes, and finding out about their construction is one of the activities we regard as geometrical. One should start with the boxes themselves, not with a discussion of nets.

Examine and experiment with boxes and packets as used for patent breakfast foods, washing powders, and confectionery. Select those whose seams can easily be opened up by the children, and ask children to bring these to school until a sufficient collection is on hand, one for each child and spares for those who spoil their work. The activity can develop as a class lesson. Give each child a box and show how it can be opened up into a flat sheet. Discuss why the box is made this way, and get the class to refold the box into its original shape.

Extend the activity by bending the card *backwards* along the folds and reassembling the box inside out. Have glue available since most children will want to stick the flaps together and take their inside-out boxes home with them. Most of these packets are machine-made. Some more expensive confectionery and cosmetics are packed in boxes which are folded using tuck-in flaps without glue, by hand: these can also be turned inside out. Both kinds of box, when thus inverted, can be decorated with paint or cut-outs.

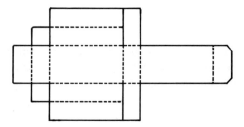

The earlier exercise in drawing round the outlines of the faces of cuboid boxes can also be extended, by labelling and describing the 'footprints' in words.

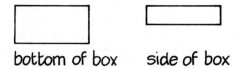

bottom of box   side of box

A short discussion can be started with questions such as,

Are the faces all different sizes?

Is the top the same as the bottom?

What can we say about faces that are opposite to one another?

Although we have adopted an entirely non-numerical approach, it is worth noting that boxes of this kind can also be used for collecting and recording measurements, but only among older children who can use millimetres or measure to the nearest centimetre. Early work in measure should be done with rods and so on, cut to exact sizes to avoid fractional measures.

42   Symmetry patterns: an introductory exercise

The study of symmetry is one of the more obvious distinguishing features of a modern course in mathematics. Symmetry, like tesellation which will be discussed later, lends itself admirably to a practical approach with the younger age groups, where mathematics easily merges with art and craft work. It also lends itself to a wide range of abilities and a wide variety of skills. We recommend an approach for this age range without any attempt at analysis. At each later stage the pupils can be referred to earlier work, repeating it only as a convenient starting point for the new ideas. The familiar ink blot pattern is an example of bilateral symmetry. The concept as such is best deferred until it can be discussed with the appropriate vocabulary. The aim here is to build up a set of experiences from which, later, the abstract concept may be derived.

The term 'ink blot' has been retained, although it is difficult to find liquid ink as such in a modern primary school. The blots are made with poster colour, allowing each child two or three colours to obtain bright butterfly-like patterns. The production of a class or group can be made up into an attractive temporary wall display.

Each blot shows the line of symmetry clearly so further discussion is not necessary. One can remark in passing that one can see where the paper was folded, and ask a child to point out this line on one of the patterns. The children can see that the picture is 'the same on both sides of the line' and the adjective *symmetrical* could be introduced in context with this meaning, although one would avoid the abstraction *symmetry*.

Repeat, using a piece of string dipped in poster colour, coiled flat but irregularly between the folded sheet of paper, and then pulled out. These activities are so familiar in the classroom that examples are not needed here.

Fold a sheet of paper in half and cut in any outline, opening the paper to get a symmetrical shape.

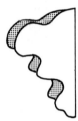 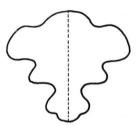

This task can be extended for the able child by asking for a drawing of the shape *before* the paper is opened. A difficult test of understanding (which often confuses older children) is to fold a sheet of paper obliquely and begin to cut it along the dotted line as shown.

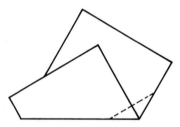

What will be the shape of the smaller piece cut off when opened out? It is not a symmetrical figure, but the child will often draw it as an 'arrow head' on the assumption that it is.

 actual    as usually drawn

Provide the children with sheets on which are duplicated one half of a symmetrical drawing or pattern and ask them to complete them. If drawn in outline it can be coloured in afterwards.

Make symmetrical patterns with gummed paper cut-outs. Here the actual line of symmetry can be drawn on a sheet of paper and children can work in pairs.

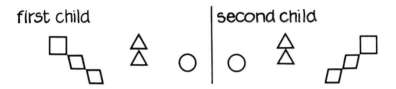

The first child leads with a shape. The other 'balances' it and then leads his own, so that each in turn has to judge the required symmetry.

Each pupil makes up a balanced or symmetrical picture using leaves, grasses, bits of fern, and the like, sticking them on paper to build up a pleasing design. (One sometimes sees dried or pressed leaves and grasses made up into permanent arrangements and used as decoration. This is not intended here, although if the children wish it the final patterns can be pressed and displayed for a few days.)

Children, working singly or in pairs, can make symmetrical patterns with coloured pegs on pegboards or coloured bands on geoboards.

It will be seen that the activities suggested are merely different examples of bilateral symmetry. Children may often notice other forms of symmetry in passing, and informal discussion at their level on almost any topic is valuable; but we do not recommend set activities devised to go beyond what has been suggested.

43   The two-part tangram: dissecting and building up shape

The tangram is an ancient Chinese toy consisting of a square board cut into seven parts according to a traditional pattern. Although any other shape or dissection is not strictly a tangram, the cutting of a square or rectangle into two parts in various ways gives a wide range of shapes when the pieces are put together. A tangram whose pieces are not symmetrical will produce more shapes when made from plain card than from coloured gummed paper, since the pieces may be turned over.

Make a two-part tangram by joining one corner of a square to the mid-point of an opposite side and cutting along the line. Mark each piece with its number for reference, on one side only.

 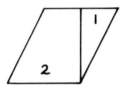 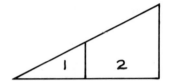

The two pieces can be put together in an indefinite number of ways unless the rule is made that only equal sides can be put together. The child can be given the two pieces and asked questions such as:

How many right angles are there in the two pieces?

Can you describe their shape?

By sliding one of the pieces on the table to join the other so that equal sides come together can you make a square?

A triangle?

A parallelogram?

(The word 'parallelogram' can be introduced informally. Some children will remember it and it then becomes part of their working vocabulary.)

A four-sided figure which is not a square?

Can you make the shapes you have just made if you turn one (only one) of the pieces over?

If not, how many different shapes can you make when you have turned one piece over?

The questions can also be given as instructions by using 'Try to. . . .' In this and the next activity with the three-part tangram do not let the child see the pieces being made by cutting up a square. We want to use the square as one of the configurations to be made up.

One assumes that the teacher is thoroughly familiar with the shapes that can be produced. This is certainly not an activity to be taken without preparation! Note in passing that the areas of all possible configurations are the same, being that of the original square. The work with tangrams can be referred to again when area is being studied.

Repeat the work with rectangles of length about twice the width cut as in the diagrams

The three cuts run

   1 diagonally

   2 from a corner to midpoint of opposite long side

   3 from a corner to cut off part of the long side equal to the width.

Number the pieces on one side only so that one can tell if a piece is turned over. By experimenting with the pieces, devise a set of questions corresponding to those already given for the square tangram. Of these three the first is most interesting because of the systematic ways in which the actual movement of the pieces as they take up their positions can be analysed, but this takes the work into more advanced study.

Note that the configurations produced include parallelograms. Here again there is an opportunity to introduce this word in context if the teacher wishes, with the rhombus seen as a parallelogram with all its sides equal. At this stage, however, 'parallelogram' is merely the name of the shape on the table: it is not the subject of a formal definition. The teacher might also like to refer to geoboards and sets of 'geo-strips' (as in Activity 37) which also provide the configurations under discussion.

44 The three-part tangram: a further dissection

As the number of pieces increases, so does the difficulty of constructing a given geometrical figure, although it becomes easier to make up a picture that is seen to represent some object or other. The three-part tangram is still a useful dissection for the abler child.

Make a three-part tangram from a square of stiff card, numbering pieces on one side only as shown.

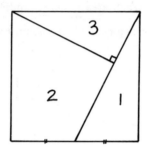

Questions can be devised as before. Typical instructions after a child has been given the pieces are:

Try to make a triangle using pieces 1 and 2.

Try to make a triangle using all three.

Try to make a square.

Try to make up a rectangle.

Try to make a parallelogram.

Try to make another four-sided figure using all the pieces.

For reference the triangle, rectangle, and the other four-sided figure are shown.

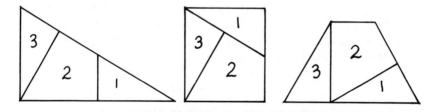

The third figure is a trapezium, but this name should be deferred until the children are ready to classify quadrilaterals by properties – a formal exercise often undertaken too soon.

45 Five- and seven-part tangrams: playing with shapes

At this stage tangrams with more than three parts are better regarded as play material. Even assembling the pieces into the original square can be frustrating for children who do not enjoy such puzzles. The connection with constant area is of great value, and it is always worth stressing that all shapes produced use up the same amount of card. We are, however, deliberately avoiding numerical computation in these activities.

The five-part and the traditional seven-part tangrams are shown below. Some teachers might wish to use the first as an extension to Activity 44. They can do so by experimenting with the parts.

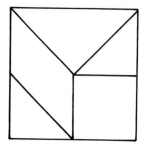 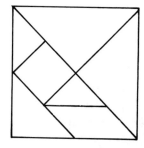

Begin by marking in the centres and the mid-points of the sides of the squares. These need to be marked out accurately. The centres of the squares are where the diagonals cross, the centres of the sides can most conveniently be found by measurement; but only more able nine-year-olds will make a good job of making tangrams, even given squares of stiff paper to start from. The most economical way is to duplicate the squares on sheets of white paper, issuing them to the pupils to cut out. When they arrive at a satisfactory 'picture' they can then paste them up on coloured backing paper for display, suitably titled.

Here we give a few shapes, dissected to show the construction. The pieces need not be numbered, since all but one in each dissection remains the same shape on being turned over.

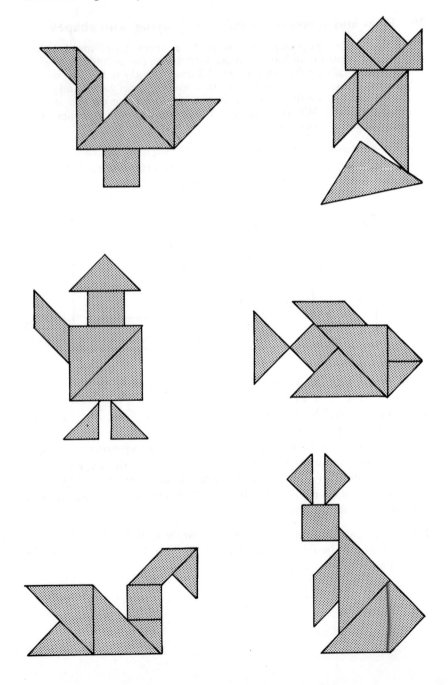

The tangram can be used incidentally as a collection of seven shapes, which the children are asked to describe. Since the aim is to construct pictures, the rule set up for Activity 42 is relaxed, and any sides can be put together with any overlap.

46 Boxing the compass: a useful skill

The angular degree, except perhaps in the informal sense of 'an angle of 90°' often used in speaking of a right angle, is too difficult a unit for the under-nines to handle easily. This can be demonstrated by giving a class lesson on the use of the protractor and then asking children to construct an angle of, say, 37°: the results are apt to be highly erratic. Nevertheless, we want them to appreciate the idea of a measure of direction. The principal points of the compass are easily grasped, and are part of everyday speech in talking of the weather. This activity relates to primary work in science.

If classroom walls face roughly to the cardinal points mark them clearly,

THIS IS THE NORTH WALL

and so on. If the room is orientated any other way it is better not to try marking it internally. Let children see a compass, preferably a large one, and show them how it is deflected by iron or steel objects, but points north and south when clear of them. If this can be done about mid-day (G.M.T.) the position of the sun gives a check on south. For most schools (not in Newfoundland or a few other places) the discrepancy between true and magnetic north need not be mentioned unless a child unexpectedly volunteers the information.

Take the children into the playground and mark out the four cardinal points, North, East, South, West, extending them to the eight principal points by adding Northeast, Southeast, Southwest, and Northwest. Some schools like to have a compass rose marked out permanently in the hall or playground. This has the obvious advantage that it is seen everytime the playground is used, and the obvious disadvantage that because it is always there it tends to be ignored. Perhaps a younger class could mark out these principal points in one corner and compare them with the permanent display painted on the ground elsewhere.

The eight points thus set up are enough, and we do not recommend, for this age range, the use of the next set of points NNE, ENE, and so on, and still less the 'by points', NbE, NEbN. These could well be part of a compass rose set up permanently for the older children, although it should be presented as for interest only. The complete system with quarter points is no longer in general use. The complexity of such a rose gives us one more reason why the younger ones should construct their own. The diagram below shows what is wanted. The circle in the centre is to allow a child to stand in the centre of it: this is important.

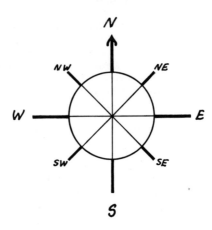

Ask the children to point in the direction from which a given wind would come, and let them hold streamers above their compass diagram in the playground to identify the wind that happens to be blowing. Get them to recite the eight points in order: N, NE, . . .

This is sometimes called 'boxing the compass', although the term usually applies to putting in all the half and quarter points on the way round.

Using a map of the locality on the largest obtainable scale, a 1 : 2500 town plan, for example, take groups into the playground and show them how to orientate the map approximately, both by using the compass and by lining up on a prominent landmark such as a church tower. Ask children to stand one at a time in the centre of the rose and point in given directions or state the bearings of distant landmarks. An expression such as 'between SE and S' can be used where either point is obviously wrong: otherwise get children to work to the nearest principal point.

47   Beginning tessellations: introduction to a later topic

The topic of tessellation, like that of symmetry to which it is closely related, is again a source of work at many levels. In the activity as given here children fit together suitable shapes that fill up a given space. We defer altogether any discussion of what kinds of shape do or do not tessellate, although of course children soon discover that a given shape falls into one or other of the two groups. Many children could go further with this work, but it is better to keep a few interesting topics in reserve.

If your school is equipped with those very useful 'half-hexagon' (or trapezoid) tables, discuss their shape with the children, asking why such a shape should be chosen. Using the actual tables if possible, with plenty of space to operate, make up some useful configurations and get the children to say what each could be used for.

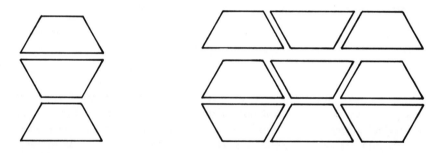

Take this opportunity to ask the question:

Is there a better way of seeing what we can do with these tables than shifting them about the school hall?

Try to get the children to suggest using cut-out card or paper half-hexagons. These are now not just arbitrary shapes but seen as models of table tops. Children can make them well enough for the purpose by drawing round plastic regular hexagons, drawing a diameter and then cutting. Each child in the group or class should have at least a dozen. The children can work in pairs. Tell them to build up any shapes they wish, although they should only put equal sides together.

By taking part in the work of pairs, try to get children to arrive at the hexagon tessellation.

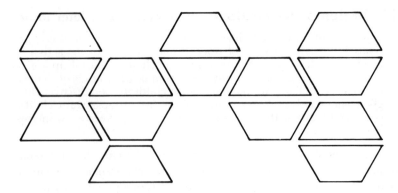

Discuss this, and relate to any hexagon pattern that may be available. Ask what other shapes could be put together, whether tables, tiles, bricks, or woodblocks, and search for examples in the school.

Issue gummed paper shapes and get some of the tessellations made up on larger sheets for display, under a heading such as:

> These shapes fit together.

The word tessellation can be used in context and is then easily learned, at least as a word to be said if not written. The word, incidentally, comes from the Latin word for a small cube as used for dice, and later for mosaic pavements. The first tessellations were made with solids, not plane outlines in the abstract.

Note that the exploration of the possible forms of tessellation is quite wide-ranging. We recommend restricting the earlier work to shapes easily available as gummed cut-outs and to these two configurations only:

> Tessellations with congruent polygons such as hexagons, squares, or parallelograms.
>
> Tessellations with pairs of shapes such as octagons and squares.

Some books restrict tessellation to tilings with congruent shapes, but here we allow different tiles to be fitted together.

Extend by using a single plastic shape and drawing round it. There can be informal discussion of the ways in which the plastic shape can be moved into a new position, if convenient referring to Activity 40 in which shapes were used to build up a pattern. The same three movements are used, since before continuing to draw round it the shape is either moved along, turned round, or turned over.

This much is easy, but it is not really possible at this stage to get children to see that any possible movement of the piece can be analysed into some or all of these three. Avoid reference to the properties of reflection in mirrors: this is a closely related topic but outside the young child's powers of analysis.

Make collections of shapes that tessellate, such as used stamps, beer mats, and labels, setting up temporary displays. Such work like other activities discussed has the incidental but valuable side-effect of getting children to carry their schoolwork into the home and enlist the help of parents.

48   Knots: a practical skill involving space and movement

Although the word *knot* has taken on a special meaning in mathematics, and although nautical interests insist on distinguishing between knots and bends, for the purposes of this activity knots are what children take them to be: a way of manipulating strings or ropes to fasten the ends or attach them to objects. The child will not see any connection with mathematics till much later, if at all, but is nevertheless working with shape, with operations involving movement and direction relative to other parts of the cord. The child is, moreover, being introduced to noncommutative operations: putting the left-hand end over the right-hand end is not the same as putting right over left. This does not need to be proved in the abstract, since some of the knots cannot be tied properly if successive operations with the cord are the wrong way round.

Obtain lengths of braided cord of 5mm–10mm diameter, dip the ends in resin glue, and trim off when dry. Only a few simple knots are needed to make the children realize that it is the shape taken up by the parts of the cord that makes knots work. It seems only reasonable to choose the few from those that might be of use to them. Practise them until they can be demonstrated to the children with confidence, and try to get every child in the class to form them successfully. If any child shows particular interest, suggest a book from the public library.

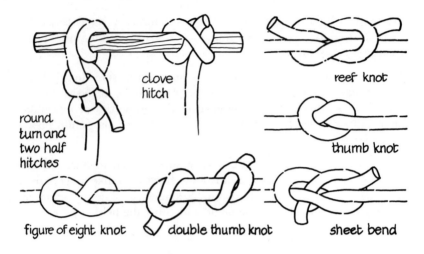

Where possible, bring the seven knots into use, even if this means devising situations *ad hoc*. Sooner or later one of them will actually be needed, and the child will enjoy showing the modest skill thus called for.

Here are some suggestions for use:

Thumb Knot

Of no use except as a stopper like the Figure of Eight, but a fundamental shape made with the cord. As with most knots, an end is put through a loop. The thumb knot is the simplest of all.

Double Thumb Knot

To join light lines. Make (and use!) a long pendulum by joining two shorter lengths of string.

Figure of Eight

Stops the end of a string from running through a hole, but does not jam tight as the thumb knot is apt to do. Make a string telephone with a long line and two empty cans. Aluminium drink cans are better than heavy tinplate.

Reef Knot

Make a cuboid box into a neat parcel with brown paper and string. This could be a very useful class session, discussing what size sheet of paper is needed for a given box, and where to make the necessary folds and tucks. This is geometry at work. It is worth showing that the reef knot will not hold if it is used to join a thin cord to a thick one. It is also liable to jam tight under strain.

Sheet Bend

Joins any two ropes or cords without jamming, and holds even if one is thicker than the other. During the industrial revolution children working in weaving sheds had to use this knot to repair broken threads, and it is sometimes called a Weaver's Knot. Get the children to tie one when this period of history is under discussion.

Clove Hitch

Use it to fasten the long pendulum cord to a suitable rod, or to construct the angle stick of Activity 33. Pulled tight over a rough surface it is likely to jam and be hard to undo.

Round Turn and Two Half-Hitches

Children will be amused at the clumsy but descriptive name. Use it for fastening a rope to a rail in roping off spaces on sports days.

Let the children examine the knots carefully after they are tied, trying to get them to see the points at which a pull on the rope becomes pressure between its parts, so that it does not slip.

49 An activity with polygons: an exercise in following instructions

This is an activity that can be followed if necessary by a large class and is self-checking. It distinguishes between three different cuts made with scissors on paper polygons, and requires the class to follow a sequence of instructions using the names which they themselves have agreed. The teacher can carry on a running commentary or series of questions, with the opportunity of introducing technical terms in a meaningful context, at a level judged appropriate.

See that each pupil has a sheet of stiff A4 paper, a ruler, a pencil, and a pair of scissors. Go through this sequence of instructions and questions, seeing that the children follow them as carefully as possible. As each is made clear, the teacher should also follow it on a check sheet, preferably an A3 that can be held up and easily seen by everybody. The actual wording of the instructions is chosen to suit the class and can be broken up into simpler steps as necessary.

Draw a line between any two points on two adjoining sides of the rectangle and cut along the line to remove a piece of the paper.

This instruction can be made clear by demonstration or by drawing on the blackboard. Now ask questions:

What is the shape of the piece cut off?

How many sides did the sheet of paper have originally?

How many has it got now?

Now repeat the first instruction and the three questions that follow. Discuss the result, concluding that each time a triangle is cut off the sheet the number of sides goes up by one. The next instruction modifies this conclusion:

Draw a line from any corner of the sheet to any point in one of the two sides that allows you to form a triangle and cut off this triangle. How many sides did your shape have before you made the cut?

How many has it got now?

This time removal of the triangle left the number of sides unchanged. Discuss the difference between the two cuts, and suggest that since the cuts are going to be used later in the lesson names are needed. Possible names would be the Plus One Cut and the Zero Cut.

Now cut off a triangle after drawing from any corner to the next but one. Discuss the loss of a side. There are now three distinct cuts, each of which removes a triangle: the third is as yet unlabelled. One could suggest the Minus One Cut. Check that all the children can perform each cut by issuing a fresh A4 sheet and asking them to do all three when told, holding up the sheet after each cut. The final shape will of course have four sides, and this could be established in advance by a question if the class is responsive.

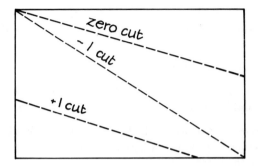

Finally, issue a fresh A4 and call for any sequence of cuts, choosing them so that the activity remains manageable, and finishing up with a triangle or four-sided figure that can easily be checked.

At one level this activity may be seen as an exercise in drawing straight lines and cutting along them accurately, but at another the discovery that there are three and only three ways of removing triangles by a cut becomes a geometrical insight. It is related to later problems with older pupils that stretch the ability to think in three dimensions. In how many ways, for example, can one cut a tetrahedron from a polyhedron and what restrictions are there? How many sides and faces are left after each cut?

50 Evaluation (iii)

We have included evaluation among the activities described because we feel that it should not be a separate process. There is, fortunately, little that has been suggested that could form the material for an examination, but at every stage what is done needs to be evaluated. What is the object of the activity and has it succeeded for each child? The introduction to the activities made it clear that our use of 'geometry' would lead its meaning away from what is usually understood by this word. All that we ask is that the child shall learn to handle objects defined by their shape and use language effectively in discussing them, ready for a more systematic approach to geometry as part of mathematical studies in the top of the junior school. Evaluation, then, discovers whether children can use geometrical words correctly in their material context. Mr. Wackford Squeers had the idea:

'C-l-e-a-n, clean, verb active, to make bright, to scour. W-i-n, win, d-e-r, der, winder, a casement. When the boy knows this out of the book, he goes and does it.'

Our version of this method would be:

Do you know what a tetrahedron is? Good. Then get one for me from the shapes cupboard and draw its face on a sheet of paper.

If more than one class is involved, the teachers concerned will no doubt like to get together to produce evaluative tasks and questions. There are three aspects of the work.

Verbal questioning, with apparatus if appropriate

Written work sheets

Practical tasks

The balance between the first two is entirely a matter for the teachers in their assessment of the children's verbal abilities. The child who can get a tetrahedron from the cupboard when asked to do so is not in *geometrical* difficulties if he falters at the name when printed.

The earlier evaluations (Activities 6 and 35) have listed words which the young child must use correctly in context. Make an extended list of those words felt to be appropriate for the actual groups of children who have worked at the activities. This list will include the earlier words such as *tall* and *short*, but must now include all those needed to discuss the activities.

Examples would be:

curved	pointed
balance	sloping
topple	rotate

Comparison of the final word list with those of reading schemes highlights one of the difficulties in teaching any subject with a distinctive vocabulary. Add to this list some of the 'technical' words as called for by the work schemes. These fall, albeit roughly, into two groups: those that are every-day words (although even then not in everyday speech) and those not often met outside a mathematical or some special context. The everyday words could include:

rectangle	horizontal
cube	vertical
sphere	diamond
pyramid	cylinder
triangle	circle

The others, less likely to be familiar to parents, could include:

cuboid	acute
tetrahedron	obtuse
hexagon	radius
equilateral	perimeter

The total list is, in effect, the vocabulary the teacher has needed in organizing the activities with the children throughout the age range. It will prove a great help in discussing the teaching of geometry with colleagues to have such an agreed list proposed by those who have taught the various age and ability groups, however organized within the school.

The next step is to devise questions and instructions, verbal or written, according to the degree of mechanical reading skill that the teacher wishes to take into account and the degree of conceptual maturity shown by the reader in understanding what is written. These would test whether a child can use and understand the words in context, or where necessary, match knowledge of the words with skill in manipulating the objects or relationships referred to. The many exercises given in the text throughout this book should suggest evaluative questions appropriate to the circumstances of age, ability, and background the teacher actually finds when dealing with children in the 5–9 range.

Appendix I Materials and Equipment

This list covers the whole set of fifty activities and is entered under three headings. The first is commercially made material as described in educational catalogues, the second lists what one expects to be normal classroom material, and the third contains material that can be collected by teachers, parents, or children. A spirit duplicator is needed for producing work sheets if these are to be used, a guillotine for cutting card and paper, and at least one large scale O.S. plan (1 : 2500) of the locality.

Commercial apparatus from catalogues

Geoboards
Plastic plane shapes
Logic blocks
Wooden cubes
Cut-out animals
Classroom magnetic compass
Gummed paper shapes
Wooden shapes

General classroom materials

Squared paper 10mm and 20mm
Dotted paper in square grid
Elastic bands
Paper fasteners
Cellulose tape
Coloured gummed paper
Poster colours
Painting equipment
Drawing pins

Tracing paper
Card for models
Milk straws
Pipe cleaners
String
Scissors
Fibre tip pens
Rulers
Paste and gum

To be collected as needed

Shells
Stones
Small dolls
Plastic cars
Balls of all kinds
Cardboard tubes
Braided cord
Labels
Beer mats
Glass marbles

Wallpaper for motifs
Gift wrapping paper
Pictures from magazines
Highway Code booklets
Road safety posters
Soft drink cans
Dowelling rod
Match boxes
Plywood and nails
Breakfast food and other cartons

Any containers or packets with an interesting shape

Appendix II

The Way Ahead

Some readers, with clear memories of their own studies when at school, will wonder if what is in this book is geometry at all. We have dealt with this point in our introduction, but it is still true that what we have produced is only an introduction, a foundation course for something that is to follow. We have prepared a set of activities that can, as an identifiably geometric part of the general work in mathematics, be used with the fives to nines. What should follow?

One of the difficulties of teaching geometry (as the word is used for the work of older pupils than we have discussed) is that many of its ideas, unknown to Euclid and his later adaptors, are fundamentally simple but capable of extension to become very difficult topics indeed. This means that they can appear both in primary school work schemes and in the opening chapters of university texts. An example that can easily be traced through book after book is Euler's famous problem of planning a route which crossed each of the Seven Bridges of Königsberg once and once only during the same walk.

The diagram that makes the problem clear is often printed.

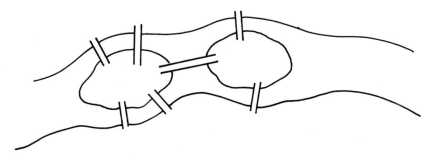

Both the problem and its solution are well within the grasp of a ten-year-old and it appears in many primary textbooks; yet it is also found in work for eighteen-year-olds and beyond.

Another example is the study of symmetry, introduced here in Activity 42. The enthusiasm with which this work is done poses problems unless there is an overall direction and it links up with what will be done later. One can find children exploring ink-blot symmetry in classes of all ages from 5–11, and then again in the secondary school. Given the development of the subject matter, repetition in itself may be no bad thing, and for some topics is inevitable. But it should have some plan behind it: it is useless if everyone concerned presents a topic as if introducing the idea for the first time.

What is needed now is cooperation, not indeed to produce a common syllabus for all schools, but at least to recognize at one level what has been done before or will be done later. It is also true that to go on from the informal work of the fifty activities needs a teacher with some knowledge of modern geometry in relation to the rest of mathematics, or at the very least textbooks very well written and annotated for classroom use. We now suggest some topics which could be in a geometrical programme for the upper part of the junior school, with children who have been given a flying start by the activities already described. This is not a syllabus: only a list of items that a fully worked-out syllabus might include, given to show how the themes of this book link up with work for older children. One hopes that this programme would in turn link up with what is done at secondary level.

Geometry 9–11

Plane shapes   Triangles and quadrilaterals – their classification and defining properties.
Angle properties of triangles and quadrilaterals.
Nomenclature for other plane shapes.
Circles – radius and diameter.

Symmetry   Extension from bilateral symmetry to multilateral.
Rotational symmetry.
Classification of plane shapes by symmetry.
Natural symmetries.

Tessellation   Tessellation with regular polygons.
Tessellation units built up from complementary shapes.
Tessellation grids.
Patterns produced by modifying grids.
Polyominoes and their tessellations.

Topology   Descriptive topology.
Unicursal and other networks.
Regions and nodes.
Topological transformations of plane figures and solids.

Solid shapes   The platonic and other solids.
Prisms, cylinders, spheres.
Open three-dimensional shapes.
Nets of solids and their construction.

Coordinate topics   Lines and configurations described by coordinate systems.
Introduction to graphical methods.
Position by bearing and distance.
Height by distance and elevation.

Transformations Collection of empirical results for various transformations.

Translation, rotation, scale transformation, and systematic distortion.

Experimental approach to reflection using plane mirrors.

Instruments Use of rulers, compasses, protractors, and set squares at introductory levels.

Patterns with instruments.

Accurate drawing of lines, angles, and simple configurations.

Informal approach to plans and elevations.

Practical

Extended use of geoboards, jointed strips, milkstraws.

Curve stitching.

Measure Use of measures of length, area, volume, and capacity in studying shapes where appropriate, but not the use of *ad hoc* formulae such as $A = \pi r^2$

This is given as a starting point for considering the way ahead. Since the need for cooperation can only be met by initiative, we suggest that any primary school devising a programme of geometry for the nines to elevens should discuss it with their local secondary schools. They should hold their ground if the inclusion of an item is criticized. They are introducing possible studies, not exhausting their content. It is also obvious that teaching from such a syllabus requires either specific mathematical knowledge or access to a suitable range of books. A well-stocked education library with opportunities for browsing will provide the best list, but as a starting point we recommend that a selection from the following should be available in schools for consultation by the staff or use in the classroom.

Bibliography

Bell, Stuart E., *Looking at solids*
  Rotation and angles
  Curves
  Transformations and symmetry
  (Vols. 3, 4, 5, and 7 of Mathematics in the Making series), Longmans, 1967/8.
Charos, Mannis, *Straight lines, parallel lines, perpendicular lines*, A & C Black, 1971.
Fletcher, D. and **Ibbotson,** J., *Geometry with a tangram*
  Geometry One (also *Two* and *Three*), W. and R. Holmes, 1965.
French, P., *Introducing polyhedra*
  Introducing topology
  Curves
Rickard, R. J., *Introducing geometry*
  (all in Exploring Mathematics series), House of Grant, 1963/4, McGraw-Hill, 1969.
Holden, Alan, *Shapes, space and symmetry*, Columbia University Press, 1971.
James, Albert, *Wheels*, Macdonald Education, 1973.
James, E. J., *Curve stitching*
  (in Mathematical Topics, Second Year, Book 2), Oxford, 1960.
Leapfrogs Group, *Dots*
  Bands
  Folds
  Pegboards
  With few words (Orange and Blue books)
  (in Network, a mathematical series), Leapfrogs and Hutchinsons, 1975/7.
Moss, Grace A., *Geometry for juniors* (Vols. 1–4), Basil Blackwell, 1960.
Nuffield Mathematics Project, *Shape and size* (2, 3 and 4), W. and R. Chambers and John Murray, 1967/71.
Ravioli, Anthony, *Adventure with shapes*, Phoenix House, 1957.
Ruchlis, H. and **Engelhart,** J., *The story of mathematics – geometry for the young scientist*, Harvey Howe, 1958.
Sealey, L. G. W., *The shape of things*, Basil Blackwell, 1965.
Trivett, Daphne H., *Shadow shapes*.
Srivastava, Jane J., *Area*
  (both in Young Mathematician books), A & C Black, 1976

Index

This index does not contain entries for topics already in the detailed list of contents unless they are needed for cross-reference.